THE FIVESQUARE CITY

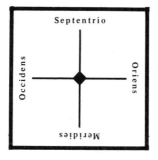

THE FIVESQUARE CITY

The City in the Religious Imagination

JAMES DOUGHERTY

UNIVERSITY OF NOTRE DAME PRESS

NOTRE DAME   LONDON

Excerpts from "Memorial for the City" by W. H. Auden are from *W. H. Auden: Collected Poems,* edited by Edward Mendelson; copyright 1976 by Edward Mendelson, William Meredith and Monroe K. Spears. Reprinted by permission of Random House, Inc., and Faber and Faber, Ltd.

Excerpts from the poetry of T. S. Eliot are from his volume *Collected Poems 1909–1962;* copyright 1936 by Harcourt Brace Jovanovich, Inc.; copyright © 1943, 1963, 1964 by T. S. Eliot; copyright 1971 by Esme Valerie Eliot. Reprinted by permission of Harcourt Brace Jovanovich, Inc., and Faber and Faber, Ltd.

Excerpts from "Wichita Vortex Sutra" by Allen Ginsberg are from *Planet News 1961–67;* copyright © 1968 by Allen Ginsberg. Reprinted by permission of City Lights Books.

The excerpt from "The Common Life" by Wallace Stevens is from *The Collected Poems of Wallace Stevens;* copyright 1942, 1954 by Wallace Stevens. Reprinted by permission of Alfred A. Knopf, Inc., and Faber and Faber, Ltd.

The excerpt from "Castles and Distances" by Richard Wilbur is from *Ceremony and Other Poems;* copyright 1948, 1949, 1950 by Richard Wilbur. Reprinted by permission of Harcourt Brace Jovanovich, Inc., and Faber and Faber, Ltd.

Library of Congress Cataloging in Publication Data

Dougherty, James, 1937–
    The fivesquare city.

    Includes index.
    1. Cities and towns—Biblical teaching.   2. Cities
and towns (in religion, folklore, etc.)   3. Cities and
towns in literature.   I. Title.
BS680.C5D68   230   79-19621
ISBN 0-268-00946-5

for j.m.d.

—who cared and did not care

Contents

Preface

MAN'S LARGEST VISIBLE CREATION, HIS MOST MANIFOLD ARTI-
fact: to name it—"city"—is to conjure with the power of words to
apprehend realities at the very limits of our comprehension. To the
Romans an intangible commonweal, to the Anglo-Normans a thing
they had only heard of in a book, "city" enters our speech always
with a charge of meaning that exceeds its literal reference to some
assemblage of women and men, streets and structures. To speak of
the city is to invoke not only that tangible presence, but also the accumulating aspirations which men have sought to realize in it and
through it. From the beginning, man has seen his city as "the center
of the world." Few discussions of urban life, whether of the physical *urbs,* or of the social *civitas,* or of their refraction in the medi-
ums of art, can avoid the city's symbolic dimension, its power to
focus our imaginations.

This book takes up the city as a symbol. To understand the city
and the intensity of our frustration with it in the twentieth century
we must consider it not only in its (frequently unlovely) experiential
reality, but also in its relation to the hope we have invested in the
city—whether we conceive that relationship as one of partial fulfillment or of nearly complete betrayal. Frequently the presence and
nature of those ideals go unacknowledged or unexamined, both by
those who indict the city and by those who would amend it, but we
cannot comprehend the city's full reality, good or ill, without recognizing that part of its reality is its spiritual freight of aspirations
and ideals. The following pages are addressed to such a recognition. *not*
sociological
I have approached the city chiefly through its refraction in the
imagination—through literature, sacred and secular, and also
through architecture and urban design when they reflect concerns
other than the simply utilitarian. Though my study is preceded by
Blanche Gelfant's *The American City Novel,* Raymond Williams's

ix

The Country and the City, and Monroe Spears's *Dionysus and the City,* my interests are generally other than theirs. We do not need literature or art to tell us how the city appears. We know that altogether too well, by firsthand experience. No set of words, however evocative, could improve on a day's direct experience of city "facts"; and to verify the accuracy of my experience, I should prefer statistics to novels. Literature is a frail vehicle for documentation. But it can become powerful when understood as the imaginative review of experience, a review that both discovers and imparts those spiritual expectations against which the city's appearance must be measured. I have paid thus little attention to books that depict, in lugubrious detail, the facts of urban life from Juvenal's Rome to Rechy's Los Angeles. My concern has been rather with those works of literature in which the measurement of reality against articulated ideals is dramatized in words, acts, and setting. I am less interested, then, in what the book of Ezekiel "says about" sixth-century Jerusalem or in Walt Whitman's record of Manhattan in the 1850s than I am in how an ideal city functions in these works and in the tension between that ideal and the cities—various and time-ridden—which their authors directly experienced. This book then is more like John Dunne's *The City of the Gods,* Helen Rosenau's *The Ideal City,* David Weimer's *The City as Metaphor,* and Lidia Storoni Mazzolani's *The Idea of the City in Roman Thought*; it is more general than the latter two, more specialized and less historically argued than the first two.

There are several clusters of symbolic association around the city. Justice is one, religious fulfillment is another; communal association and secular power are others. Four faces of the one city, each implies the others. This book examines the city as a religious symbol and, in some chapters, as a symbol of power. Therefore some familiar venues of the literary-city circuit, like Plato's Republic, More's Amaurote, and Joyce's Dublin, are left unvisited. It seemed best to omit, or only to glance at, those works where the city is a figure of justice or community and only peripherally connected with religious values.

Doubtless there are many other omissions as well: parochial blanks, works and languages and whole literatures I *should* have known. I am most at home in that tradition called "western," which leads to, and has been the main shaping force for, American writing—and also for American ideals of city living. And my book's religious perspectives are, at base, those of American Catholic Christianity. (Chapters 4 and 5 may suggest why I acknowledge such parochialism.) My contacts with other literatures and other faiths, however, encourage me to believe that my parochialism affects more my choice of examples than the ground of my argument. If I can call these cities "archetypes" without thereby annulling the possibility of further discussion, then they may be called archetypes.

The first chapter describes the holy city as it developed, in Judeo-Christian scripture, into an image well attuned to expressing sophisticated religious experience. The second chapter discusses the manifold City of God conceived by the medieval imagination. Chapter 3 examines a symbolic architecture that attributes divine power to the princes of this world; 4, mass society as a counterfeit of the holy city; and 5, a mode in which genuine religious communities might exist within the actual, historical city. Each chapter asks whether its version of the holy city must disvalue that "other" city—manifold, historical, sensibly present—where human life goes on or whether it allows the religious imagination to dwell in that city as well. My argument is that visualist, spatial images of holiness tend to occlude the "secular" city, while auditory, time-bound images help to reveal it. First and last, the holy city stands at the fifth point of the square, "the center of the world": the aspiration of this book is to lift that center from private or ethnocentric holiness within an eternal city to an open and communitarian religious presence in the secular city of man.

the point of his ringing conclusion: the power of God's grace, + the call to establish + support religious presence

Acknowledgments

LIKE ANY CITY, *THE FIVESQUARE CITY* STANDS ON LOST FOUNDA-
tions; at least two other books preceded this one, one promised but
never written and the other excised from these pages in the interest
of coherence and economy. Planning, construction, demolition,
and reconstruction have occupied a dozen years; I am grateful to
those who kept faith through that process—to friends, to my family, most of all to her to whom the book is dedicated. I am indebted
to the University of Notre Dame for a semester's leave in 1972,
when the work was planned, and for routinely assuming the costs
of typing and duplicating the manuscript; to Dean Isabel Charles
of the College of Arts and Letters for inaugurating the Frank
O'Malley Prize competition that brought this book to the Notre
Dame Press; to James Langford, John Ehmann, Ann Rice, and
Richard Allen of the Press, for good advice and sympathetic criticism throughout the process of publication.

Preliminary studies for the unwritten book appeared in *Cross
Currents* in 1966 and in *Continuum* in 1968: my thanks to Justus
George Lawler for his patient encouragement of my work—however
TFSC-2 may have disappointed his hopes. A much-extended ver-
sion of the treatment of Washington in chapter 3 was published as
"Baroque and Picturesque Motifs in L'Enfant's Design for the
Federal Capital" in *American Quarterly* (copyright 1974 Trustees
of the University of Pennsylvania). I am grateful to the editors of
AQ for permission to reprint from that essay. The view of Saint
Augustine in chapter 2 appeared, in a much different form, in *Au-
gustinian Studies* in 1979 as "The Sacred City and the City of
God": I appreciate the editors' permission to publish this version
of that work. An excerpt from chapter 4 appeared in *Alternative
Futures: The Journal of Utopian Studies* (Winter 1979–80) as
"Whitman and the Prophets of Mass Society": my thanks to the
editors of *AF* for permission to reprint it here.

1: The City at the Center of the World

HERE, AT THE CENTER OF THE WORLD, GLEAMING ABOVE THE featureless plain, rises the holy city. In the eastern wall there are three gates; in the western wall there are three gates; in the southern, three; in the northern wall, the same. Within these gates men dwell in peace and concord, for they are all of one mind. From the chief gate in each wall a broad thoroughfare extends to the city's center, where another wall surrounds the royal precinct. Through those gates only priest and noble may pass. Inside is the king's palace, splendid in gold and marble, its wall encompassing apartments, gardens, and great halls. Nearby, at the city's exact center, stands the pyramid of heaven; at its top a temple to the great god, and within the temple a chamber, open only to the skies, where the king and the high priest enter once a year at the spring equinox. Beyond that room, beyond the temple, beyond the palaces, beyond the sacred precinct, beyond the city's twelve-gated wall, beyond the great and fertile plain, beyond the passes in the encircling mountains, lie the regions of the barbarians, demon-worshipers, gabbling in outlandish tongues, contentious and torn with factions, forever testing our defenses at the passes, forever sallying across the plain against the inviolable walls of our holy city, here, at the center of the world . . .

This image of the holy city, a shrine at its heart, begirt with walls, encompassed by barbarian nations, has floated for a long time through the human mind. Sometimes this city is, indeed, a city, and we can discover in its historical, literary, or architectural record the aspiration of mankind to fix upon the earth the corporate, physical embodiment of its dream of social concord, immortality, and godlike perfection. Even in those records, though, and in the imaginations that aligned the temples and traced the walls' circum-

1

ference, we can see that embodiment dissolving into a symbol through which its artificers gave form to some spiritual reality, perhaps not much like the tissue of stone and wood and men and women that we name "city." Let us look first at actual cities, or designs for cities, which men have called holy, and then at some scriptural versions of the holy city, in which the imagination has sought to present something less tangible than a shrine within a rampart but no less worthy of reverence. At times the holy city is a symbol of spiritual tranquility, an inwardness grounded on communion with God. Or it may be set against an opposing, unholy city, to represent religious experience as a choice between alternative measures of life. Or it may represent a goal which, though unattained by those who conceive it, yet directs their actions and serves as the bond of their fellowship. Each of these versions of the holy city implies its devotees' taking an attitude toward that other city—not holy, not profane, but simply secular—which is the city we experience, the city where we live "in time."

In societies where the sacred is indistinguishable from the magical, the legendary foundation of a city is a religious act. Its site is determined by a theophany, the manifestation of some god to a mortal. And the city then continues to serve as a place where the immortal or divine intersects with the mundane. The devotee who enters its gates approaches "the center of the world," sometimes a miniature of the cosmos laid out in a quadratic geometry emphasizing the points of the compass and usually having at its fifth point, the center, a shrine or tower where the union of earth and heaven, man and god, is ritually consummated. The city is surrounded by a consecrated wall, for space that has been made holy must be manifestly distinguished from that which has not; the world where time decays and all things lapse into confusion must be discriminated from the place where immortality rests. In the magical mind the wall is an adjunct of holiness. "Long before [walls] were military erections," writes Mircea Eliade, "they were a magic defence, for they marked out from the midst of a 'chaotic' space, peopled with demons and phantoms, . . . an enclosure, a place that was organized, made cosmic . . . provided with a 'centre.'"[1]

Many of Eliade's examples come from technologically innocent cultures whose sanctuaries are single houses with a central pole:

American Indians, Asian herdsmen, Australian aborigines. Yet there have been great theocratic societies with the social and technical resources to enact whole cities on that design. Often a single encompassing wall was not enough, so the city developed a concentric structure, each ring more holy and more difficult of admission. Such an architecture focuses on the ritual figure of a priest-king, who alone may enter the holy of holies, who from its eminence commands all the city's space, whose acts realize the citizens' dreams, who sums the city up and is in symbol its only responsible person.

Peking, for example, China's ancient northern capital, is a nest of walled cities: the ideogram for "wall" also means "city." Construing the cosmos as four quarters around a center, the Chinese conceived their homeland as the "Middle Kingdom" and Peking as its sacred center, its site and orientation determined long ago by astrologers and geomancers. Its fortresslike gates were designed, by height and position, to keep demons from entering the city. Within that wall lies an "inner city" which the Ming emperors in the fifteenth century modeled after the legendary T'ang capital at Ch'ang-an. And within it is the walled Imperial City, the enclave of the emperor's residence and the empire's administration. Within that, the Forbidden City, into which only members of the imperial household were admitted, where a symmetrical arrangement of gardens, halls, and palaces leads to the Hall of Divine Harmony, the center of the world, the emperor's sacred throne room. Elsewhere in the city was the Temple of Heaven, an explicit geometrical model of the universe: within a square wall, with gates at the cardinal points, a circular wall surrounded a series of three concentric marble rings ascending to a terrace where the emperor came at each solstice to offer sacrifice to heaven. The square represented the earth; the rings rising above it, the heavens. "The Imperial Palace and the Temple of Heaven," writes a recent historian of Peking, "manifest the central Chinese belief that *all* power, therefore *all* good, comes from a nonpersonal heaven and is transmitted solely through the person of the emperor."[2] Within the city both temple and palace might serve the same symbolic purpose, for a sacred universe can have many "centers," wherever man gains access to the divine.

Pre-Columbian America used the same design. Tenochtitlan,

the Aztecs' holy city, stood on an island in Lake Texcoco in the Valley of Mexico, its site determined by an omen of the god Huitzilopochtli. Causeways, oriented north, south, and west, linked it with the mainland; from the bridgeheads streets extended to the center of the city, to a great plaza ringed with palaces and temples. In the plaza were the Aztecs' immense calendar stone and the "stone of war," a central milestone from which armies were dispatched to the quarters of the empire. Within a double wall in the square reared the city's tallest pyramid, its truncated top bearing temples to Huitzilopochtli, god of fire and war and the summer sun, and to the rain god Tlaloc.

Aztec theology, like that of the Chinese, postulated a universe of four quarters and a center. Each quarter was dominated by a creator god linked with an element, an allegorical significance, and a color: north, earth god, death, black; east, rain god, fertility, red; south, fire god, uncertainty, blue; west, wind god, knowledge, white.[3] At the center (and elevated above the plane of the four quarters) was the sun god, who held the contending elements in balance; the Aztecs supported him in his struggle by bloody sacrifices from atop their pyramids.

The archaeologist Laurette Séjourné argues that this fivepart figure was the symbol of harmony in both macrocosm and microcosm:

> The most familiar Nahuatl [Aztec] symbol is composed basically of four points—the sign for solar heat—placed about a centre. We have seen that the number 5 represents the centre, and that it is also the point where heaven and earth meet. . . . This five-fold figure, or quincunx, is also the precious jewel symbolizing the heart, the meeting-place of opposed principles.[4]

Eliade compares this city to the *mandala*, an image used in Buddhist meditation; and C. G. Jung, discussing the seeming universality of mandalas as symbols of psychic wholeness, points out their occasional representation as a geometric city. Noting the recurrence of square-in-circle or circle-in-square motifs, Jung argues that they are attempts to convey geometrically the perfect union of material and spiritual, time and eternity, body and soul.[5] In the cosmological imagination, the city is simply the enlargement of the temple or sanctuary and stands as the intermediate term in an iso-morphic universe where the city-temple is at once the microcosm of the universe and the macrocosm of man. And so the city's unanimity may symbolize not only the manifest perfection of the wheeling heavens brought down upon the earth, but also the desired perfection of the human beings who enter the city: temperance, serenity, wisdom, immortality. The way to the center is the path of purification, and to arrive at the holy of holies is to experience visionary illumination. This city has both a political symbolism and a significance for the individual psyche.

The mandala-city, its holy walled enclave quartering the cosmos and excluding chaos, is essentially an image drawing its power out of the subconscious. Like all archetypes it has great force, witnessed by its agelong survival in art as well as in the psyche. But, as Jung points out, its ultimate meaning is inexpressible, for it is the reflection of an inability in conscious life to state a goal or to help oneself.[6] When built in stone, the ring city conveys a sense of its citizens' private helplessness, as it collects their aspirations in a common center for the priest-king to enact and allows them to share that enactment in their imaginations. When built in words rather than in stone, this city usually represents a condition which its author regards as the fulfillment of man's aspirations, the completion of human personality, through an escape from the ambiguities and tensions of ordinary life—life in the flesh, life in the real city, life in time. Sometimes these aspirations are social, the city representing an ideal of harmonious collective life. Often, though, it shades off into a symbol of spiritual unity attained within the single soul.

Jerusalem, sacred in the midst of the profane, unanimous in spirit, figures prominently in the Old Testament narratives and lyrics attached to the figure of David. In their nomadic years the Jews depicted Yahweh as a citybreaker, like the other great kings of the ancient Middle East, humbling the baalim, the king-gods and god-kings of the Canaanite cities. They were plainly hostile to cults founded on stabilized holy places and their attendant sacral kings. Later, when David and Solomon amalgamated Israel, Judah, and Canaan into one kingdom with a throne city, Jerusalem, God became the protector of that city. This development is negotiated in scripture by a series of dreams, prophecies, rituals, and prayers in which the nomadic Yahweh accepts a permanent "house" like the king's house and adjacent to it in the citadel on Zion. The king himself is provided with a parallel biography, transformed from shepherd boy to urban monarch.

In the psalms, Temple, Zion, and Jerusalem are a nested, isomorphic "center of the world" where the sky god makes His earthly home. They are the symbol of Israel's unity and integrity. Most of the psalms are monologues spoken in the person of the king, whose mind fuses religious and political realities. Like the David of the historical books, who is rendered as an isolated man barely in control of his own family, his army, his nation, and his frontiers, the psalmist finds himself at the calm center of a cyclone of cosmic, political, and personal chaos. He attributes his interior tranquility and strength to the power of God and to his righteousness before Him: God is his "shield," his "rock,"; he "takes shelter" in Him. Outside this ring lie "the nations"—chaotic, undifferentiated, rebellious, unclean—and the demonic powers of nature. The imagery of siege is the structural base of Psalms 46 and 48, where it so dominates the poems that they may seem merely anthems to Israelite theocracy:

> God is inside the city, she can never fall,
> at crack of dawn God helps her,
> to the roaring of nations and tottering of kingdoms,
> when he shouts, the world disintegrates.
>   Yahweh Sabaoth is on our side,
>   our citadel, the God of Jacob![7]

However, the sense of interiority and unity is not so much geopolitical as it is psychological and religious. It can be expressed in other metaphors as well—the familiar "Lord is my shepherd" of Psalm 23, the analogy between God and thirst-quenching water in Psalms 42 and 63, the recurrent images of harmonious music and of God as a just judge or a loving father. All these reveal the psalmist's consistent experience of God as an encompassing peace, a simplicity of spirit, an ultimate freedom from external agitations. His most frequent metaphor for this experience, nevertheless, is his fortress on the heights of Jerusalem, Zion:

> Those who trust in Yahweh are like Mount Zion,
> unshakeable, standing forever.

> Jerusalem! Encircled by mountains,
> as Yahweh encircles his people. . . .
>
> Ps. 125:1-2

Other psalms make the symbolic quality of the city more explicit. Betrayed by a friend, David allegorizes his state as that of a city:

> Sorrow and Misery live inside,
>   Ruin is an inmate;
> Tyranny and Treachery are never absent
>   from its central square.
>
> Ps. 55:10-11

The ideal monarch, says Psalm 101, would banish such enemies from "the city of God." The irruption of rebels and enemies within the "wall" is here a psychological threat, and this gesture of purification is religious and penitential rather than political. Like other assertions of Zion's harmony, it does not square with historical fact. David preferred to have his political enemies close at hand where he could watch them. Rather it applies to the personal spiritual life the convention of moral unanimity which magical religion applied to the city: harmony, self-containment, the exclusion of what is threatening and alien.

In the psalms, then, the cosmological city achieves explicit symbolic significance. Most of the conventions of such cities are evident: the "sacred" exclusion of the unclean, extended into imagery of siege and war; the immortality and unanimity of those who dwell in the city; and the city's enclosure of a shrine where man may enter—in fact or in imagination—and attain access to the divine. On the one hand these symbolic qualities are turned toward the hoped-for unity and dedication of the newly forged Davidic kingdom. But more importantly, the psalmist has discovered in the city a symbolic macrocosm for an individual's religious sense of shelter and peace in communion with God.

> Yahweh, remember
> what the Sons of Edom did
> on the day of Jerusalem,

how they said, "Down with her!
Raze her to the ground!"
Destructive Daughter of Babel,
a blessing on the man who treats you
as you have treated us,
a blessing on him who takes and dashes
your babies against the rock!

Ps. 137:7–9

In the world of the prophets, as in this late psalm, the days are past
when David and Solomon struggled to assert the hegemony of Jerusalem against a rabble of malcontent Palestinian chieftains. The
context of their writing is the grinding together of great empires in
the Middle East, which Israel and Judah experienced as a series of
invasions culminating in the conquest of Jerusalem by Babylon,
and the deportation of many of her people to the Chaldean capital.
In the prophets the conflict between Zion and the undifferentiated
nations of the gentiles—between chaos without and harmony and
peace within—has sharpened into the antithesis of two clearly defined antagonists, Jerusalem and Babylon. Each city has a role to
play in God's design; for though both are sinful and proud, one is
destined for final ruin and the other for rebirth.

The prophets call into question the ethnocentric religious
righteousness of the Zion psalms. In the eyes of Isaiah, Jeremiah,
and Ezekiel, man either may trust in human designs, or trust in
God. To the Jerusalem of their day, the decadent Davidic kingdom, they announce an anti-politics: put faith in your walls, your
alliances, your idols, and you will be destroyed; put faith in God
above, and though the city may fall, you will live, and later God
will restore it to you. To Babylon (or Tyre, or Damascus) they announce the passive subversion of the politically helpless: you have
only your walls and your idols to put faith in; they crumble, and
you will be destroyed.

The recurrent literary strategy of the prophets is the juxtapo-
sition of imagination and experience. In the midst of the thriving,
idolatrous, jeering city, they see the city dead: ramparts broken,
buildings burnt, the streets full of dead, women humiliated and
raped, the temple profaned, and the ruins finally a lair of jackals
and an object of wonder to passers-by. In the midst of those ruins,

or in exile, they envision a new city, resplendent, wealthy, blessed by God and faithful to Him. Thus the prophet sees not only two cities, but two versions of each city, one version a realistic or even satiric view of experience, the other that of apocalyptic vision. One takes the two cities as they are; the other depicts them as they will be in the future, when God's judgment has been enforced on those who have mocked Him, and His mercy bestowed on those who have trusted in Him. The prophet then construes his images bifocally, not only in space, but also in time. Manipulating images of these two cities, and the alternative temporal versions of each, the prophet fulfills his twofold task of accusation and consolation.

When the present city, the city of experience, is Jerusalem, the prophet may use a realistic mode to reveal that it is no longer a city "centered" on the Temple and the Law—

> You have as many gods
> as you have towns, O Judah.
> You have built as many incense altars to Baal
> as Jerusalem has streets.
>
> Jer. 11:13

—and is therefore a city out of touch with its history, for the Temple and the Law have become magical talismans rather than ever-present reminders of the special covenant between Israel and God, on the basis of which the rightness of all private and public acts must be judged. The prophet uses his visionary mode of writing to reestablish this sense of covenant history, referring both to the past and to the future. He calls into his hearers' memories a familiar story: God once made a covenant with Abraham and his descendants, a covenant reiterated, in varying forms, to Moses and to David and Solomon, but made always through them to the people as a whole. How does that covenant stand in the collapse, imminent or accomplished, of the Davidic kingdom and the dispersal of its people? When Zion lies desolate, palace and temple in ruins, who is responsible?

Measured against this religious disposition of the events of history, the current crisis appears no longer political but moral, the occasion of God's apocalyptic judgment. Though the prophets are often shown addressing the kings of Judah and Israel and proffering advice which seems political in character (as Isaiah counsels against alliance with Egypt against Assyria), they address the kings not in their civil power but as moral representatives who stand for the people. As a rule the prophets do not subscribe to the myth, still evident in the historical books dealing with those years, that the king's acts alone merit the vengeance or the mercy of the city's god. What falls upon the city collectively has been deserved by each of its citizens.

Only by insisting on universal responsibility, derived from the universality of personal sin, can the prophets raise in the individual mind the question of a coherent moral life and so the question of one's personal relationship to the covenant and to the law; for in their recurring agricultural image Israel is being winnowed, reduced to a "remnant" made up of those in whom fidelity to God—and God's own fidelity—have been confirmed. To Isaiah, Assyria's war machine (which he describes with unseemly relish) is only the rod of punishment, the flail winnowing away the chaff. Since the prophet's first function is to awaken in his people a sense of their deviance from the will of God and to encourage repentance, he treats the war as an act of correction and selection, either threatened or already executed, administered by God in His care for His nation, properly affecting every member of that nation.

A second function of the prophet, more evident after the city's fall and the deportation to Babylon, is to console and consolidate a community deprived of its geographical base. When the present city is Babylon, he uses the realistic mode to satirize its idol cults, reminding his people that God is still *their* god. The apocalyptic vision now consoles them with promises of a better future for them and ruin for their conquerors. This latter consolatory role takes an even more profound view of sin. The sin of Jerusalem is not, of course, David's adultery or Solomon's idol worship, but neither is it simply the private vices of all the citizens. Rather it is the communal sin of pride and self-sufficiency, a sin which every city expresses by its very construction and function, and for which all will be punished one day:

> The arrogance of men will be humbled,
> Yahweh alone shall be exalted,
> on that day.
> Yes, that will be the day of Yahweh Sabaoth

against all pride and arrogance . . .
against all the lofty towers
and all the sheer walls,
against all the ships of Tarshish
and all things of price.

Isa. 2:11–16

The composite effect of these prophecies is to measure against impending apocalypse the vanity of human efforts to build paradise anew within the city's walls:

The wide ramparts of Babylon
will be razed to the ground,
and her high gates
will be burnt down.
Thus the labouring of the peoples comes to nothing
the toiling of the nations ends in fire.

Jer. 51:58

Again the prophets' apocalyptic imagination recovers the city's willfully forgotten dimension of time. Worship, commerce, building, lovemaking, entertainment: the activities of the city all must be conducted as though they would endure forever. Yet in the devastation of war they will vanish utterly, and their ruin reveals the nullity of man's efforts to manufacture happiness. Their point, however, is not the universal pessimism of Ecclesiastes and other Near-Eastern wisdom writings, but an assertion of man's dependence on God. To trust in the works of man is not only vain; it is perverse. It expresses a loss of faith in the care and generosity of God.

As far as the prophet is concerned, the ruin of Babylon and Tyre is final. Their fall expresses simply God's vengeance, not His wish to correct and to purify. But Jerusalem, though it has fallen because of the same prideful reliance on walls and idols, will be renewed by God for the "remnant" of the Jews who recognize His sovereignty. It is the prophet's task to summon those who can hear, those whose imaginations are open to see cities which are not at hand—first a ruined city (in contrast to those whose minds are filled by the present Jerusalem, confident in its walls and its treaties), and beyond that a restored, messianic city (in contrast to those who foresee only ruin, having no trust in God). It is these whom the prophet calls to "return," not from literal exile but from a preoccupation with the present which has stifled their imaginative awareness of the covenant both as a law in the past and as a promise extending indefinitely into the future.

For Isaiah, the remnant is those who survive God's winnowing in the sack of Jerusalem. But Jeremiah and Ezekiel revise his message: if God is with those alone who have His law written in their hearts, then the true winnowing takes place not in the chance slaughter of war but in the temptations of a dominating alien culture. God's purposes then are best served not in a physical "Zion," where mere habitation and loyalty may define the Jew, but in Babylon, where to be a Jew is to resist—not just the cult of Bel and the pogroms of Haman, but also the opportunities to become not Daniel the Judean but Belteshazzar, prince of the satraps of Persia. Thus the prophet's call—turn away from your reliance on human power—is transferred from Isaiah's context of defense policy in a city under siege, into the quotidian realm of subjugate resistance. Jeremiah writes to the exiles in Babylon:

> Yahweh Sabaoth, the God of Israel, says this to all the exiles deported from Jerusalem to Babylon, "Build houses, settle down; plant gardens and eat what they produce; take wives and have sons and daughters; choose wives for your sons, find husbands for your daughters so that these can bear sons and daughters in their turn; you must increase there and not decrease. Work for the good of the country to which I have exiled you; pray to Yahweh on its behalf, since on its welfare yours depends." (Jer. 29:4–7)

In Babylon the issue is clarified as it could never be in Jerusalem, where kings persist in attributing to Yahweh their own designs. The exiled Jew can look at the silverplated gods of Babylon and say to the Lord *in his heart,* "Master, it is you that we have to worship" (Bar. 6:5). He may serve the state loyally, as Daniel-Belteshazzar does, but not its gods; may support the state's civil order and benefit from it, but seek not its power.[8]

Jeremiah counsels the deliberate acceptance and exploitation of ghetto status as the way to a religious purity unattainable in Jerusalem:

In the country of their exile they will take all this to heart and acknowledge that I am the Lord their God. I will give them a heart and an attentive ear. They will sing my praises in the country of their exile, they will remember my name; they will not be stubborn any more. (Bar. 2:30–33)

As the law of Yahweh is internalized "in the heart" of each of the faithful remnant, so the remnant itself assumes a corporate identity within the foreign city, differentiated by and organized around the service of God. The exile community gives form and membership to what was invisible in Isaiah's Jerusalem by attracting to itself those who are truly faithful. Those who are not may begin the process of assimilation; the city's gods are at hand, and the king has offered a royal robe and a horse and a diadem to those who serve him wholeheartedly. The idea of "remnant" then combines a heightened realism about the "immortality" of Jerusalem with a determination to make theological sense out of the status of what was evidently the most culturally and religiously vital segment of Judaism, those in exile in Babylon. The remnant, however, is not defined simply by its alien status and its fidelity to God—that is, by a translation into spiritual terms of the ancient sacred precinct, devils without and god within. The Judean remnant in Babylon survives (while the Samaritan diaspora disappears) because it keeps faith in a vision of Jerusalem.

The messianic promise, of course, is expressed in many images. Just as the "remnant" is sometimes represented not as a ghetto but as a seed, often the restored Israel is seen in pastoral images of sheepfolds and rich harvests. Or the emphasis is on the messianic king or on the extent of the new Israel's spiritual or political hegemony. Often, as the prophecies of accusation spoke of the "infidelity" and "prostitution" of Jerusalem, the consolations present the nation as the bride of Yahweh. But the orienting vision of the prophecies of consolation is a new city with a new temple, whither the remnant will some day make its way across the desert. This renews the imagery of Exodus while giving the "promised land" of ancient nomadic Israel the focal point appropriate to an urbanized community familiar with the cultic and political use of a city as the climax of a ceremonial procession. The most sustained evocation of the City Beyond is from the latter part of Isaiah. It draws on three related images: a royal progress, a king's triumphal approach and entry into his palace city; the city as a goal for those seeking commercial, legal, or religious requital; and finally the city as a place of refreshment for travelers in a semiarid land. In Lewis Mumford's familiar terminology, the sacred city here is not a container but a magnet, a city far away, experienced not as a comforting enclosure but as a prospect. The imagination conceives it not as a succession of more and more holy arcana, but as a cynosure, its splendor drawing and uniting those who have eyes to see it.

An exiled people is a group whose spiritual center lies beyond its own physical limits. It has a center "within" only in its shared imagination of that City. One cannot go to Jerusalem without first imagining the way there. Nor can one resist the seductions of Babylon without imagining oneself to be on the Way to Jerusalem. The remnant survives because the Way and the City live in its imagination. Isaiah wishes to create in the communal imagination a vision of Jerusalem Afar, as a symbol of unity such as the actual city once had been. To it return and in it unite the tribes of Israel scattered by schism and conquest (Isa. 11:10–13; Ps. 122). For the exiles in Babylon, their City was manifestly *not there*: they, or their fathers, had seen it in ruins, and such it still was. Nor was the Way a route they were free to travel. Both the Way and the City, then, derive their magnificence, their attraction, their power to bind a people together, from their reality in imagination rather than their actuality.

Like Isaiah, Ezekiel lives in a double world, part an actual city —Jerusalem or Babylon, places of disunity—and part an imaginary world of restored unity; and the unitary state always involves an explicit removal, by "the hand of Yahweh," from one to the other. As the scattered bones come back to life, as Israel and Judah are reunited, so the book that began with a divided Jerusalem and with the homesick exiles on the banks of the Chibar in Babylon (and with a prophet present to both, despite the distance in space and time) concludes with the elaborate geometric unity of a visionary Jerusalem conceived as a temple precinct atop a mountain, refreshed by a great stream of water rising from the Temple. The Jewish people, seen in their ritual ascent to this city, are restored to unity; they are a "remnant" no longer. By conceiving Jerusalem as the goal of a Way, the prophet extends his hearers' imagination to another place and to other times, both past and future. They must think of themselves as moving in time, and thus judge their actions in relation to the continuity of God's covenant with them. So the holy city, as a reality imagined rather than experienced, may serve as a symbol of religious process, and not simply of fulfillment and an escape from time.[9]

The visionary mode suggests that, as Jerusalem's fall was moral rather than political in cause, so Jerusalem will be redeemed not for new political hegemony but rather as a manifestation of the mercy of God as striking as the rainbow of Noah, and on the other side of a cataclysm in history as powerful as the flood in canceling the effectiveness of mortal wills: the Day of the Lord. That day of judgment will restore the harmony between merit and reward, it will see the righteous vindicated and the proud destroyed. Exterior disharmony led the psalmist into creating an interior city-sanctuary of timeless peace and order. In the prophets, religious fulfillment is projected in time, in images of one city in ruins and another city in triumph. These are "real" cities, not allegorical figures, but the visionary mode has polarized them as evil and good by relating them eschatologically, that is, to the forthcoming judgment of God. And the same visionary power sustains its people through the years of exile—of a life seemingly cast out from God's presence—by sustaining in their minds an image of their city restored.

The sacred city, its unity and immortality set against an encircling demonic chaos, may have begun as a magical device in an age of religious naiveté. But in the hands of psalmist and prophet it becomes an explicit spiritual symbol, distinct from the "facts" about Jerusalem, and available to express sophisticated religious ideas. In the development of Christian, as with Jewish, iconography, we can trace a process by which the city is transformed from a hostile reality to a religious symbol dissociated from particular, historical cities.

The cosmological city, grounded in the ancient geopolitics of magical and military power, would seem incompatible with the Christ of the gospels. The synoptic evangelists show Christ as a countryman who meets his most formidable and daunting opposition in towns and cities while moving steadily toward the capital city, where the customary usage of prophets is execution. He draws both his followers and the symbols of his ministry from the rural world of food production—agriculture, viniculture, and fishing.

The parables present a world which, with some exceptions, divides into a benignant countryside of good shepherds, generous vineyard-owners, and abundant harvests, and a hostile urban scene of vengeful kings with armies and torturers, conniving stewards, and locked and guarded doors. Further, in his escape from the ritualism and political messianism of contemporary Jewish belief, Christ sought to free his followers' minds from the traditional pairing of sacredness with place, dismissing the significance of Jerusalem and its Temple, and answering Pilate's question about the location of his "kingdom" with a denial not only of his own political power but of the Roman's as well. So the traditional response of Christ's followers to the city has been to present it not as a simple reality but as an allegorical figure for some spiritual truth.

Doubtless because it often applied to their actual situation, Christians quickly took up the scriptural image of God's faithful as a community of exiles within a foreign and unsympathetic city. Drawing again on the imagery of the exodus, and on those psalms in which the enduring City of God is not Jerusalem but the heavenly city, Saint Paul defines the Christian as a weary tent-dweller moving toward a heavenly house (2 Cor. 5:1-3). "Our homeland," he says again, "is in heaven" (Phil. 3:20).

The imagery of exile was also grounded in the contemporary reality of the Roman empire. The ancient world determined a man's citizenship by his ancestral city. The conquests of Rome, destroying the religio-political autonomy of the Mediterranean cities, left their populations in a semistateless condition where only Roman citizenship—inherited or acquired—was of value.[10] One was part of the Roman *imperium*, enjoying its protection, or one was nothing. The early Church often made the resolution of these anxieties its symbol: "Once you were not a people at all," Saint Peter writes to an audience of Jewish converts "living among foreigners" throughout Asia Minor; "and now you are the People of God" (1 Pet. 2:10). "You are no longer aliens or foreign visitors," Saint Paul tells the gentile converts at Ephesus; "you are citizens like all the saints" (Eph. 2:19). That is, they had found a new citizenship in the City of God, a city inaccessible to the statekilling expansionism of the Roman *imperium*, and yet present, as a "church," within the gates of Ephesus or the towns of Cappadocia. In the Epistle to the Hebrews, the City Beyond is adapted to the Christian message.

Writing to a community of Jewish Christians, exiled from Jerusalem by the insurrection against Rome, the author seizes upon their specific weaknesses—homesickness for Jerusalem and nostalgia for the old ways of Judaism—as a symbol of the real meaning of the faith. He attributes to Abraham and all his lineage the hope for a holy city felt by the Babylonian exiles, identifying as the character of their faith their status as "strangers and nomads" persevering amid trial and privation in the expectation of entering, someday, "a city founded, designed and built by God" (Heb. 11:10, 13). He then transfers this expectation out of the bounds of time, saying that as God's glory in Jerusalem eclipsed that displayed on Sinai, so the glory of the New Jerusalem will eclipse that of Solomon's city (Heb. 12:18–22), the immortal priesthood of Christ supplant the earthly priesthood of the Temple (Heb. 7:23–28). Therefore to seek a place of rest nearer at hand is to disobey God as some did in the exodus (Heb. 3:7–4:11): "there is no eternal city for us in this life but we look for one in the life to come" (Heb. 13:14).

The Apocalypse of John, which begins with a warning to Christians not to rest in the cities of their exile, concludes with a vision of the City Beyond, adapted from Ezekiel and the other prophets and from the cosmological tradition of the geometrically perfect city. The splendor of that Jerusalem was to make it the lodestone of the medieval image of a holy city. But the prophet does not enter the city. It is a prospect, not a fulfillment. The Book of Revelation, taken as a whole, is a Christian extension of the mission of Jeremiah, offering consolation to a subjugate people. For Christians newly troubled about their relationship to the Roman empire, this work offers an account of the triumph and eventual humiliation of Rome, veiled in the visionary conventions and images of Jewish apocalyptic writing: trumpets, seals and bowls, horsemen, grotesque beasts, symbolic women and angels, Gog and Magog, the ruin of "Babylon" and the revelation of a new and heavenly "Jerusalem." This imagery is not a cipher to obscure the author's treasonable opinions. Rather it is a device, commonly used in Daniel and in some of the minor prophets, to mask the seam between accomplished history and a future for which the writer devoutly hopes. More importantly, this imagery subsumes the chaotic events of the first century into archetypal patterns, giving manifold significance to the first general persecutions of the Christian Church.

To call Rome "Babylon" established for this audience a historical context for the crucial issue of the persecution by Domitian: the worship of false gods, specifically the cult of the ruling state. In those parts of Isaiah and Jeremiah written in exile, satires on idols are frequently part of the oracles announcing the imminent fall of Babylon. Written long after the return to Jerusalem, the book of Daniel has for its historical theme the Babylonians' efforts to compel the Jews to worship their state gods, while its visionary passages relate those efforts to the contemporary persecution of the Jews by Antiochus Epiphanes, who abolished the cult of Yahweh in the Jerusalem Temple and set up a statue of the Olympian Zeus there. In the days of Roman tolerance, the Apostles and Saint Paul could counsel the Christians simply to keep clear of idol worship. But Domitian changed all that by proclaiming that the emperor, as incarnation of the *imperium,* that divine idea of universal order, was himself divine and must be worshiped, on demand, by all who enjoyed that order as residents of the empire. The Christian, whose faith told him that his Christ is king, now heard that his emperor was god. One king had invaded the other. The author of Revelation sought to give his audience the same imaginative consolation that Isaiah had given the Jewish exiles: the toppling of the idols, the restoration of rightful kingship, and the punishment of the city which had committed the great sin of cities, making itself a god, accountable and inferior to none. And John's vision of plagues, invasions, and final holocaust shows Rome humiliated by the Parthians, just as Isaiah anticipated the punishment of Babylon by Cyrus.[11]

Beyond establishing this historical parallelism, Revelation construes the breach between the empire and the faithful of Christ as an allegory of the absolute separation of good and evil. Isaiah and Jeremiah had treated Babylon as an instrument of God, who encompasses the siege, deportation, and exile in His purpose to punish and correct His people. John of Patmos sees Rome as the instrument of another personal spiritual force, Satan, whose power may come ultimately from a concession of God (Rev. 20:7) but whose actions do not further the purposes of God, but rather parody and seek to subvert them. Thus he describes the inquisition made by Rome against the Christian Church as an episode and type of the war between good and evil, between King Christ and King

Satan, extending across all history. As in the Jewish apocalypses, war implies the complete disjunction of two powers, the settling of allegiances on one side or the other. Christ, as king, might require from his followers the same loyalty professed in the Roman soldier's oath (*sacramentum*): never to desert, even to the point of death. John repeatedly encourages his readers to maintain their loyalty to the kingship of Christ, while reporting the equal steadfastness of those who curse the name of God. Each city ritually excludes the other's citizens (Rev. 13:16–17, 22:14–15). A man must choose. So whereas Jeremiah could counsel his fellow citizens to surrender to the Babylonian army, and even encourage the captive Jews to cooperate with Babylon in secular matters, the Christians are urged to resist and to escape (Rev. 18:4). For as each man has chosen, so will God choose, in John's version of the Day of the Lord:

> Happy are those who will have washed their robes clean, so that they will have the right to feed on the tree of life and can come through the gates into the city. These others must stay outside: dogs, fortune-tellers, and fornicators, and murderers, and idolaters, and everyone of false speech and false life. (Rev. 22:14–15)

Thus not only the current persecution, but the eschatological perspective of John, focusing on the day when God will judge everyone according to the life he has lived, allows him to divide human society into two exclusive groups, each a "city" with a common spirit.

In the New Jerusalem, time will be no more. The city's geometrical perfection symbolizes a spiritual and physical perfection that transcends and terminates the flux of time, the lapse of all earthly things into ruin. The Christian's life in time can be phrased, as we have seen, in the imagery of an exile's journey toward that city. There was, however, an alternative image in scripture, equally urban, by which the process of spiritual life might be phrased. This was the imagery of building. Construction images are common in the New Testament, deriving from Christ's identification of himself with the "cornerstone" of Isaiah. They are found in both Peter's and Paul's epistles, though they refer not to a city but to a single building, the new temple of God—which is Christ, the community of his followers, or the individual believer, depending on the context of the metaphor. In the second-century *Shepherd* of Hermas, the building, now identified as the Church, is called a tower, *pyrgos*, a term with connotations of urban defense. In all these metaphors, the reference of "construction" is dedication to Christ and developing solidarity with him and with all other Christians. It is an image of corporate religious experience.

The fourth-century poet Prudentius, in his *Psychomachia*, extends the construction metaphor into the building of a city and combines it with the ancient image of the holy city under siege to create a sustained allegory presenting the personal moral life as a spiritual warfare. It is difficult for Prudentius to yoke together this image of siege with that of the symbolic holy city in a way that serves his purpose, which is to depict moral life as an internal conflict, a spiritual civil war between the forces of a divided will.[12] Still, he succeeds in establishing that his city is a symbol of the human soul, clarifying the microcosmic implications of "Jerusalem" in the psalmist and in Ezekiel, in Hebrews and in Revelation, by withdrawing all identification with any actual city.

The poem depicts the combats of seven Virtues with their corresponding Vices. These are waged on an open "field" near the Virtues' "camp." This camp is much like the Roman *castra*, a rectangular work atop a hill, its tents protected by a palisaded earthen rampart. There reside "the peaceful Senses," who take no part in the fight. The spiritual conflict is a successful sally by the Virtues against "the cruel barbarians who had besieged the dwellers of the holy city."[13] Evil is externalized, and routed. Prudentius's image does not suggest that the Christian struggle is *within* the self and *against* the self; or that it is a struggle that never ends.

The poem's conclusion extends Prudentius's allegory from "warfare" to "city," depicting a series of events and rituals which invoke the ancient civil magic of orientation and enclosure. As the Virtues reenter their camp, they experience a pagano-christian theophany, "the face of the Thunderer smiling on their stainless ranks, and Christ in the heavenly citadel rejoicing for their victory." The leaders of the Virtues, Concord and Faith, then direct a temple to be built in the center of the camp. Though Prudentius takes his description of the temple from the nested geometry of Ezekiel and the splendor of Revelation, the actual building ritual is one which

Roman augurs might have used four hundred years earlier to transform Prudentius's native Saragossa from military camp to city—that is, from profane space to sanctuary. In the Roman ritual the *templum* was first the cosmic square, inscribed on the ground, to bring down upon the featureless earth the cosmic harmony of heaven. In Prudentius's poem, Queen Faith measures out a square with a golden rod, and jewelled walls are set up, three gates in each side, oriented to the points of the compass. Within this temple there is an inner chamber, a dome on seven pillars, called a ciborium or baldachin, where like an emperor "mighty Wisdom sits enthroned."

In dedicating this sanctuary, Faith asks, "What use is it to defeat the earthly army of Sin, if the Son of Man, coming down from his heavenly citadel to the city of the purified body, finds it unadorned and without a splendid temple?" Prudentius's city then is a trope for the soul of the single Christian in his struggle against sin. Not only do the didactic passages at beginning and end make that identification, but his description of the four-sided temple links it with the nature of man "which a four-fold power animates," and with the four ages of man, each associated with a cardinal direction—"the dawn of boyhood, the burning fervor of youth, the full light of maturity, the cold north wind of old age." Prudentius elaborates on the microcosmic meaning of his numerology—"in each of the four phases of life, [man] approaches the altar of the heart through a triple gate"—and so sets within its twelve-gated square sanctuary a seven-pillared circular tabernacle, to symbolize with circle, square, and mystical numbers the attainment of perfect harmony.

This similarity of his city to the New Jerusalem of Saint John is, however, only superficial. The New Jerusalem is primarily a symbol of the Church, the community of the faithful, "militant" in time and then "triumphant" at the end of time. Prudentius's city is a figure for the religious life of the single Christian, first in moral struggle and then in the peace of justification. Saint John emphasizes his city's inclusiveness—"the gates of it will never be shut . . . and the nations will come, bringing their treasure"; and in Revelation the arcane is effaced forever: "I saw that there was no temple in the city. . . . The throne of God and of the Lamb will be placed in the city, His servants will worship Him, they will see Him face to face." This image of religious freedom and communalism is quite different from Prudentius's more esoteric holy city, which excludes a demonic exterior world and sets a temple within a wall and within the temple a shrine called the "holy of holies." His city presents no human collectivity at all, secular or sacred, but rather is a figure in a moral allegory representing personal holiness attained through the ascetic way of inwardness, progressive purification, and the externalizing of disharmony and evil. The unanimity of this city stands for the tranquility of the sanctified soul. In the hands of this Christian allegorist, the range of the city image has been extended to include, as it had for the psalmist, a symbolic representation of the personal spiritual life.

With the completion of Judeo-Christian revelation and the writings of the earliest Church Fathers, the holy city was no longer just a physical place, a magical "center of the world." The holy city's magic, indeed, had always lain in the dimension of the imagination: in a knowledge of inner shrines and spiritual mysteries perceived by the mind's eye rather than by the body's. To render that holy city in words was seldom simply to describe its walls and temples as they were—or even as they should have been. Through the words of scripture, that city became a shrine, or the rival of a hostile city, or a far-off cynosure. It symbolized spiritual fulfillment; or the conflict between life centered on self and life dedicated to the service of God; or religious life as stabilized and communalized by a completion still remote in time. The words of scripture gave the holy city a manifold symbolic reality.

With the spiritual and physical decay of Rome, and with the withdrawal of Constantinople and Jerusalem to the frontiers of Christendom, an age began which could not have conceived the holy city as a physical, magical center. But the legacy of scripture assured that the city had not vanished. Saint Augustine, meditating on the manifold reality of the inspired word, found in that city, and in its earthly counterparts, a symbol that pervaded all history. And the architects of that age, drawing likewise on scripture, restored the physical holy city in the microcosm of the Christian church.

2: Heavenly City, Earthly City

> *Even now, in this night*
> *Among the ruins of the Post-Vergilian City*
> *Where our past is a chaos of graves and the barbed-wire*
>   *stretches ahead*
> *Into our future till it is lost to sight,*
> *Our grief is not Greek: As we bury our dead*
> *We know without knowing there is reason for what we bear.*

W. H. Auden, "Memorial for the City"

SAINT AUGUSTINE'S THEME IN *THE CITY OF GOD* IS A MORAL CON-
flict like that presented by Prudentius, but his dominant metaphor
is a contrasted pair of cities, like Isaiah's. Augustine founds his city
image on an antithesis developed from Christ's teaching, "No man
can serve two masters." Like Prudentius, he speaks of the moral
life as an internal warfare: "We can know no perfect peace so long
as there are evil inclinations to master. Those which put up a fight
are put down only in perilous conflict; those that are already overcome cannot be kept so if one relaxes, but only at the cost of vigi-
lant control" (19. 27).[1] But this war is not a siege against demonic
chaos, as in Prudentius; it is a war between two states, the "kingdom of God" which Christ announced, and the kingdom of Satan.
To Augustine these are first of all states of soul, the one a condition
of self-denying love for God and one's neighbor, the other a condition of hatred, egotism, and self-sufficiency. Between these, the
life of the spirit is poised. Following the tradition of urban imagery
for the human soul, Augustine describes each state as a *civitas*, a
term conveying both "city," and, because of the ancient state's reliance on the spiritual significance of its capital, "commonwealth."
    But Augustine was to experience great difficulty in controlling

the imaginative power of the metaphor he had chosen. Any effective metaphor must have a wealth of associations in its literal meaning, as a ground for its figurative significance. Yet the writer must struggle with and limit those associations, to align them with the ideas he wishes to convey. His City of God is now David's shrine, now Isaiah's adversary to Babylon, now John's cynosure at the end of time. It is somehow both Paul's symbol of corporate belief and Prudentius's symbol of private spiritual asceticism. Augustine's uneasy metaphor of the city reflects a crisis in meaning experienced by the postclassical Roman city. The very term *civitas* was in a state of transition. Classical Latin had carefully distinguished it from *urbs*, the physical agglomeration of walls and buildings. In Augustine's day the two terms were becoming synonymous.[2] This shift in definition reveals how the late Roman world was losing its grasp on the network of ancient pieties, rituals, and civil duties that had constituted a city's spiritual unity, its *civitas*. But in Augustine's mind the city was still bound to its local cult; it still reeked of its Baal. He seizes this moment of linguistic change to proclaim a new spiritual sense of *civitas*, founded on a new principle of commonwealth, faith in Christ. But his imagery depends, in a variety of ways, on the symbolism of the *urbs*.

Augustine did not regard his city image as a matter of artistic choice, issuing from his private fancy. It was to him the necessary image. He had not chosen Rome as his adversary in the first half of his treatise. His opponents in controversy had done so, and so had the civilization for which they stood, focusing its imagination and resting its beliefs on Rome as a culmination of the ancient view of the city as the home of the gods, the center of the world, the residence of perfection and immortality. To attribute these qualities to the city was not the nonce metaphor of a Plato, nor the extravagant compliment of a Virgil, but a reality which the city's religious cult, as well as its polity, sought to actualize. In the polemics of the opening pages of *The City of God*, Augustine is quite willing to accept this view of Rome as microcosm:

> I am undertaking nothing less than the task of defending the glorious City of God against those who prefer their own gods to its Founder. . . . I must speak also of the earthly city—of that city which lusts to dominate the world and which, though nations bend to its yoke, is itself dominated by its passion for

domination. From this earthly city issue the enemies against whom the City of God must be defended. (1. 1)

"Rome" then is not just a metropolis in Latium, nor even just the former capital of a political empire. It is the symbol of a religious cult and of a spiritual orientation antipathetic to the Christian God.

Nor, in Augustine's view, was *civitas* his arbitrary choice for the contrary spiritual orientation.

The expression, "City of God," which I have been using is justified by that Scripture whose divine authority puts it above the literature of all other people. (11. 1)

Of human society there are only two kinds, which according to our Scriptures can properly be called "cities." One city is that of men who live according to the flesh. The other is of men who live according to the spirit. (14. 1)

The latter city then is "Jerusalem," not so much the metropolis in Palestine as the heavenly throne city celebrated in the Zion psalms. Augustine cites these psalms as the specific scriptural authority for describing the way of the spirit as a city, the City of God. This too is not to him simply a metaphor, but a reality; for, as we shall see, scripture is not just a historical book, but is history itself.

In 410 Alaric's Visigoth army sacked Rome. This stroke, the warmaker's citykilling act, was done mainly for its symbolism, since the Roman government with whom Alaric was quarreling had moved to Ravenna eight years before.[3] Augustine began *The City of God* as a polemical response to the pagan Romans' interpretation of the sack as punishment for their having tolerated and even accepted the Christian God, to the neglect or humiliation of their old divinities. It was also a willful and polemical attempt to dispatch the whole idea that holiness depends on a magical arrangement of the three dimensions of space.

So Augustine's immediate use of the old, unitive sacred city is a negative one, turned against the pagans' belief in the holiness of Rome. In his view, a new sense of time has uncentered this "center of the world." The old cosmologies had used the city's stable and harmonious form to manifest on earth the power of the heavens. The evangel found this power instead in the history of the Redemption, a sequence of time which, for Augustine's exegetical imagination, had a symbolic richness in comparison to which the ancient city became "shadowy" and unreal. Furthermore, Rome's own history testified to its uncentering. Eighty years earlier, Constantine had established his new capital on the Bosporus—a city, Augustine remarks, without pagan temples and images of the gods. This deprived Rome of the focal clarity which for centuries it had given to and received from the empire. The civil government of the western empire had moved out in 402. Politically Rome was no longer the axis of the empire; in the west, it had no successor, as political centralism was itself expiring. *The City of God* announced to the half-pagan, half-Christian world of the early fifth century that the myth of divine Rome was also dead. Its sacred precinct was violated, its unity broken, its gods defeated and dead. The space it occupied had returned to the profane.

It was fitting that Augustine should carry out of the city's wreckage a couple of lines from the *Aeneid*, from a prophecy spoken by Jupiter on behalf of the Roman descendants of Aeneas, promising them "*imperium* without limit" in space or time. Augustine exhorts his reader:

> Reach out now for the heavenly country. . . . In that land there is no Vestal altar, no statue of Jupiter on the Capitol, but the one true God, who "will not limit you in space or time, but will give an empire universal and eternal." (2. 29)

Trading again on the contrast of pagan Rome with Christian Constantinople ("no Vestal altar") as well as on Virgil's expression of the Roman longing for the immortal and universal, Augustine announces that the city as a unitary symbol is dead: that since human history began there have been two cities. No magical ceremony, no act of imagination can efface a division which is the essence of history. In Adam and Eve, he says, mankind finds the unity of a common nature and the harmony and peace of a blood relationship. But with their sin came duality, the disharmony of body and soul that causes death and the struggle of "spirit" against "flesh" that leads to sin. The great diversity of men and nations can never again be subsumed in paradisal unity. All men in history must choose between Christ and Satan; and at the Last Judgment God will consign all His creatures to one everlasting city or the other. One city is unholy, even demonic. The other is holy, having in fact some of the qualities of the old ring-city; but its holiness depends not on excluding time through the magic arrangement of its physical dimensions, but on its relationship to the fourth dimension of time, to the history of salvation, and to the final disposition of saint and sinner at the moment when eternity begins.

Augustine's strategy in the first ten books of his work is to depict within Rome, even before its fall, those very evils which the sacred city had sought to wall out from itself. Theologically and ethically, Rome was not order but chaos, a legion of gods, a swarm of philosophies. Demons occupied its shrines. Its promise of immortality—in civil memory, in the endurance of the *imperium*—was the shadow of a shade. Where then should men look for the urban epitome of their ideals? To the heavenly Jerusalem, and in some degree to its earthly incarnation, the Church. There immortality is to be found, and peace, and unanimity in the kingship of Christ.

However, Augustine does not often treat his holy city as a shrine of peace at the center of a hostile and disorderly world. His image of two antithetical cities has more in common with the moral vision of the prophets, especially Isaiah and Jeremiah, and with the Revelation of John:

> Wherever His Church will be (and it will be among all nations, "over the breadth of the earth"), there is to be the camp of the saints and the beloved City of God. There will she be, surrounded by all her enemies . . . , girt with the appalling magnitude of that besetting, hemmed in, straitened, and encompassed by the pressures of that mighty affliction; but never will she give up her fighting spirit, which Saint John expresses in the image of a fortified camp.[4]

His vigorous writing extends the scriptural image of two warring cities into a panhistorical reality, an enduring conflict between loyal angel and fallen angel, between Israel and its foes, between spirit and flesh, between those who follow the way of Christ and those who do not, between the Church and the powers of the secular world.[5]

This antithesis allows him to create an imaginative harmony between the events of profane history, the events of scripture, and the life of the single soul. But it is a meaning that can only be discerned by reading back from the end of the story. He grounds his binary analysis of human behavior on God's final distribution of mankind into the two everlasting kingdoms. He confesses at the outset of his book that "on earth, these two cities are linked and fused together, only to be separated at the Last Judgment" (1. 35). But, he continues, "with God's help, I must turn to what I think ought to be said about the origin, progress, and respective destinations of the two cities, in order to exalt the glory of the City of God, which by contrast with other cities will gleam the more brightly." Augustine felt that the apparent confusion of the two cities could be resolved into the clarity of opposed light and darkness—not so much because God would inspire his own writing, but because the things of this world contained in themselves an allegorical meaning which, by using an eschatological perspective, he could trace out.

In an explanation of why God tolerates evil, Augustine writes, "He meant the harmony of history, like the beauty of a poem, to be enriched by antithetical elements. . . . Just as antithesis lends beauty to literary style, so, in the antitheses of history, there is a rhetoric not of words, but of facts, that makes for beauty" (11. 18). Augustine takes God as an artist in facts (and with compositional habits like his own): physical facts then stand for other, less tangible realities, just as word sounds do; the servant of God, recounting history, will offer an exegesis of it, as of a poem. He aligns his word-creating human imagination, so far as he can, with the reality-creating mind of God. God has so construed not only the words of scripture, but also the acts of history, that they are full of spiritual meaning: one may legitimately apply to the facts of history methods developed for the exegesis of inspired words. The best and highest sense of things is their reference to the kingdom of God. And an event which "symbolizes only itself" is self-contained and dead.[6]

As an exegete Augustine seems to have distinguished clearly only two meanings: the "literal" historical deeds and persons presented by the narrative, and an "allegorical" or "spiritual" meaning. His contemporary John Cassian discriminated three spiritual interpretations, one moral (applied to the life of the individual Christian), one allegorical (discovering, in the narrative, types of the life and teaching of Christ and his Church), and one anagogical (concerning the end of time and the final kingdom of God). Cassian's theory of the fourfold sense of scripture dominated scriptural exegesis throughout the Middle Ages, and was applied by Dante to secular writing as well. It is useful to apply these discriminations to Augustine's reading of history. For his "literal" Rome and Jerusalem are related to these different interpretations in differing ways; and the adequacy of the city symbol varies too, according to what significance is intended.

Augustine clearly regarded scripture (like history) as written for the sake of "allegorical" interpretations. However, he was often at pains to affirm and elucidate the facts of the biblical narrative. Erich Auerbach includes Augustine as one of the earliest of those "figural realists" through whom he traces the dominant stylistic tradition of western literature, a style in which the randomness and density of sensory reality is sifted, arranged, and interpreted in accord with the author's discovery of the "significance" of persons and events—their capacity to yield, to the imagination, references to other persons and events or to mental or spiritual realities. Augustine's city is no fictive Atlantis, a myth invented to render an idea. For him the symbolic quality of Rome and Jerusalem comes not from his own literary act but from God's providential direction of the facts of history. And no man, he says, may legitimately advance a spiritual interpretation, however edifying, which corrupts or flouts those facts (17. 3). While it is clear that Augustine regards true "reality" as found in the heavenly city alone, he does not discount physical reality so long as it is used to the knowledge and praise of God.

As an allegorist, however, writing a moral lesson through the exegesis of the facts of history, he can admit into his account only a very limited and stylized view of reality. Auerbach comments on Augustine's *The City of God* and the new postclassical field of discourse it helped create:

> The figural interpretation of history emerged unqualifiedly victorious. Yet it was no fully adequate substitute for the lost comprehension of rational, continuous, earthly connections between things, for it could not be applied to any random occurrence. . . . And so vast regions of event remained without any principle by which they might be classified and comprehended—especially after the fall of the Roman Em-

pire, which, through the concept of the state which it exempli-
fied, had at least oriented the interpretation of political occur-
rences.[7]

With Augustine's two cities, the relationship between "figure" and
"reality" fluctuates treacherously. At times figural considerations
so dominate reality as to distort it unrecognizably. At other times
reality so invests the image as to warp its figural significance.

Most of these problems occur because the division between
the personal and the collective senses of *civitas* coincides with that
between its figural and its historical senses. Augustine's image of
paired cities is effective for phrasing contrary orientations of the
personal moral life, aversion from God or conversion to Him. Not
only the physical but the theological center of *The City of God* is
books 12–14, where, having concluded his polemic against Rome,
and before commencing his history of mankind, he speaks of the
human will and its power either to embrace the evil within itself or
to turn to the good beyond itself. The dichotomy of two hostile cities also speaks effectively to eschatological meditations on God's
everlasting confirmation of men's attitudes at the end of time. But
beyond the personal sphere, and before the Day of Wrath—that is,
in the world where historical cities really exist—this polarized image becomes a rack on which the complexities of human institutions and relationships may be broken. To apply Cassian's terms:
while the "moral" interpretation asks a man only to judge himself,
and the "anagogical" leaves the general judgment to the infinite
wisdom of God, the "allegorical" application of the image requires
Augustine (and his heirs) to make judgments in history, discerning
"prophetic" parallels between the warring cities, Jerusalem and
Babylon, and the cities, states, and institutions of one's own time.
Prudentius, in the *Psychomachia*, used the city image in a simple
moral figure to represent the life of any individual Christian. But to
write a history, Augustine must apply his "cities" to actual human
collectivities—as though the various and relative good and evil of
all such groups and individuals might be easily reduced to two homogeneous and intolerant *civitates*, as though it were possible to
find earthly institutions which adequately embody one city or the
other.

It is only by adverting to the ancient myth about the homogeneity and unanimity of the city that we can understand why "city" could be used as a figure for the absolute separation of good and evil. Real cities, modern or ancient, could not have been so homogeneous. We know from the *Confessions* that Augustine was fully aware of the heterogeneity of late-fourth-century Rome. Yet this is not the Rome that figures in *The City of God.* Rather it is Rome allegorized. Augustine's figural view of history does not permit him to look closely or comprehensively at the physical reality which carries significance. In allegory, the physical characteristics of the image are reduced to only those appropriate to the controlling idea. For Aesop, what matters about the cock is his boisterous pride, and the lion his strength. Bunyan's City of Destruction contains a house, a field, a slough (of Despond), and some of Christian's family and neighbors. So the social confusion and cultural diversity of the ancient city—apparent in writers like Petronius, Juvenal, and Tacitus, who adopted the inclusive, randomizing, disorderly mode of satire—are aspects of reality to which Augustine's imagination was not open in *The City of God.* The city enters his writing not from his experience but through its figural identification with Babylon. That Christians helped govern Rome, that Christians (including Augustine) as well as pagans were appalled by its fall to Alaric—these historical realities would only confuse the allegory he is tracing through time. That the actual or "secular" city, with its dynamic mixture of good and evil, idealism and immorality, might have given him an equally cogent metaphor for the Church on earth, in time—such an idea simply falls outside his view of reality.

Augustine's two *civitates* are spiritual societies; repeatedly his work insists that on earth, in human institutions, the two cities are inextricably linked and fused together. However, he was irresistibly led to associate the two cities with visible human groups. His figural view of reality, which made it possible to trace God's city in ancient times through the lineage of Abraham, suggested that a similar localization of the city should be possible in modern times also. And the image of the city itself would not submit to a purely spiritual role. The term *civitas* added to spiritual unity its accumulating associations of physical propinquity and architectural incorporation. It was inevitable that the two cities would come to signify sacred worship and profane life, state and church, two counterkingdoms competing for power in the postconstantinian Roman empire.

For Augustine's City of God did not symbolize a religion of pure interiority: "The life of virtue should be a social life," he observes; it is as axiomatic to him as it had been to Saint Paul that persons are not saved individually but as part of the body of Christian believers. The city metaphor, like the temple built up of many stones, is an image of corporate religious identity. Christianity is a faith stabilized by a community and a tradition of doctrine, and so distinguished not only from paganism but from heretical Christian belief as well. It is truly a *civitas*, according to his definition—"a multitude of reasonable beings voluntarily associated in the pursuit of common interests" (19. 24). To stress the unanimity of Christians in their faith, he draws upon the ancient convention about the city, that it is a single moral entity, sharing a common destiny, and summed up in the person of its king, "for He is the source of our happiness and the very end of all our aspirations. . . . We offer Him our allegiance—for 'allegiance' and 'religion' are at root, the same" (10. 3).

Part of that allegiance, in the Christian tradition, had been the expectation of a millennial kingdom of the faithful, as promised in Revelation. Discussing Christ's kingship over the earth, Augustine says that the Church, even though it has not yet been purified of its unworthy members, "here and now is the kingdom of Christ and the kingdom of heaven" (20. 9). The cosmological twinning of temple and city applies in Augustine's figural world as well. Apropos of Psalm 96, a poem for the dedication of the Temple of Solomon, he writes "The house for the Lord, the City of God, that is, the Holy Church, is being built over all the earth" (8. 24). In his vocabulary the ambiguous denotation of *civitas*, spiritual and physical, is complemented by that of *ecclesia*, at once the assembly of the faithful and the place of assembly. The City of God is not grounded on physical location, as in the ancient city, but is rather a spiritual and universal kinship. Yet it lives, in history, in "the Church" and in "churches." In the *Confessions* he tells of a man who had reached the point of assent to the teachings of Christianity, saying "I am a Christian in my heart," but who refused to enter the church building. "Is it walls that make Christians?" he asked (8. 2). Yes, says Augustine, walls *do* make a Christian, for they enclose the congregation before whom the convert must profess his faith, with whom he worships, and to whom he must appeal if he breaks faith. The City of God, here and now, is "the Church," an enclosed social institution with a hierarchical organization, thresholds of membership, and an incorporative and symbolic meeting place. To enter it is to step out of the confusion of profane space and time, into a cosmos of manifold significance.

Augustine's urban image then allows him to emphasize the collective nature of redemption and righteousness in the Christian faith. To make this point, he boldly reads the apocalyptic division of mankind back into time, while acknowledging that it is not entirely accurate to do so:

> Our city must remember that, in the ranks of its enemies, lie hid fellow citizens to be, and that it is well to bear with them as enemies until we can reach them in their profession of faith. In like manner, the City of God itself . . . harbors within its ranks a number of those who, though externally associated in the common bond of the sacraments, will not be associated in the eternal felicity of the saints. Some there are who, covertly or overtly, join the enemy in abusing the God whom they have promised to serve.[8]

When Augustine presents his two cities as correlative historical realities, he does some disservice to the plenitude of the spiritual life he seeks to illuminate. The passage just quoted, with its implications of treason, mutiny, and the fifth column, is not very satisfactory for representing the complex psychological experiences of conversion and of lost faith. Contrast that passage with Augustine's account of his own conversion in the *Confessions*: it illustrates Auerbach's criticism of figural realism as reductive and insensitive in rendering complex processes in time. Augustine's autobiography is a record of his resistance to the pressure of irreversible time. Each chapter records the protagonist's loss of some comfortable illusion, and his ensuing sense of desperation, followed by the narrator's exposition of the imperceptible development toward Christ caused by the loss. "Time is not inactive," he remarks early in that book (4. 8). But time *is* inactive in the earthly City of God, for everything in it is polarized with reference to the end of time. Augustine's image does not illuminate the temporal stages of the spiritual life, the varying degrees of surrender to the will of God. And it can only acknowledge indirectly the actual condition of the early-fifth-

century Church. Since the conversion of Constantine, and especially since the antipagan edicts of Theodosius, a mixture of secular
and spiritual motives was common among those who presented
themselves for baptism. The Church's task for the next 1500 years
was to make the most of such mixed motives. Yet there is little that
Augustine can say of this, except to complain that "reprobates . . .
crowd our churches," to be winnowed out only at the Last Judgment (18. 48).

His system of figural interpretation allows him to say that the
Church *is to be* the City of God; it is an allegorical shadow prefiguring an eschatological reality, the heavenly Jerusalem which is to
come (15. 2). The City of Man, however, simply *is*, here and now.
God has written nothing directly in its history, as He has in the history of the City of God, and so its significance is far more problem-
atic. Discriminations are more difficult to make. One term, *civitas
terrena*, "earthly city," denotes both the system of secular manage-
ment of the affairs of men, its goals and ideals restricted to man's
natural being, and also the moral way of selfishness, license, and
diabolically inspired violence. And the physical image of both is
the city of Rome, in its legislative ideals on the one hand and in its
final moral decadence on the other.

Augustine follows John of Patmos in applying to Rome the
epithets which the prophets had given to Babylon. Thus Rome, in
Augustine's scheme, enters the imagination only insofar as it can
be identified with the City of Self, in opposition to the City of God.
Apart from this opposition, Rome signifies nothing. The continuity of its history, expounded by writers without divine inspiration,
promises nothing. Its efforts to manufacture happiness are as absurd to Augustine as Babylon's were to Jeremiah. Augustine did
not mean to denigrate Rome's civil order, which the citizens of
God need during life as much as anyone, having no mandate to replace it with another system of peacekeeping. But he had no exegetical system to distinguish, in "historical" Rome, between an "allegorical" Republic and a "moral" Babylon; no critical apparatus to
distinguish proper limited civil functions from secular absolutism
and from municipal cults which he saw as demon worship. Both
are simply *civitas terrena*, the earthly city, the City of Man. Therefore he must dismiss the best of pagan thought together with its
most abominable superstitions, its most idealistic affirmations of

monotheism and human brotherhood along with its blood sacrifices and obscene dramas.[9] "Even the wise men in the city of man
live according to man, and their only goal has been the goods of
their bodies or of the mind or of both" (14. 28). And secular virtues, whether personal or social, are to him based on the principle
of war for the sake of peace which he regards as the essence of the
earthly city's search for order.

Further, since Rome attains significance only by figural identification with Babylon, and thus by its opposition to Jerusalem,
Augustine can only posit a relationship of hostility between the two
cities. God has written history in antitheses. The opposition of
Christ and Satan, Jerusalem and Babylon, spirit and flesh, is also
the opposition of *ecclesia* and *civitas terrena*. The natural state of
earthly existence is warfare. The City of Man, forever racked with
civil strife and international belligerence, is also at war with the
temporal City of God. For the City of Man can tolerate any cult or
opinion which does not question the integrity of secular purposes,
but cannot tolerate a society that does. And the Church, during its
earthly sojourn, is forever at war with Satan and his agents, and
also with any civil state that presents itself as the apex of human
spiritual aspiration:

> The heavenly City . . . has been unable to share with the
> earthly city a common religious legislation, and has had no
> choice but to dissent on this score and so to become a nuisance
> to those who think otherwise. . . .
> So long, then, as the heavenly City is wayfaring on earth,
> she invites citizens from all nations and all tongues, and unites
> them into a common society of travelers. (19. 17)

Here, then, is a further reason why the Kingdom of Heaven must
be prefigured by a citylike Church. The City of God differs from
the City of Man because of its orientation toward a principle and
person beyond itself. The City of Man, on the other hand, is self-
inclusive and self-justifying. Evangelized man has been invited out
of the earthly city; he is no longer simply the product and the servant of the power of this world. It is right, therefore, that the City
of God should appear on earth like a city, offering a focus for
those who choose no longer to look to themselves, or to the City of
Man, for "the center of the earth." If the object of a *civitas* is to se-

cure peace, to extend an *imperium* based on law, then the Church offers allegiance to an alternative "city," with a higher and more lasting peace, and an *imperium* based not on necessarily defective human justice but on the love of God and man, and on an appeal to the absolute justice of God. Here Augustine anticipates the interminable struggle of Christ's followers to liberate men from Caesar, a struggle often confused or muted when Caesar was baptized and bishops came into the purple. This was to be the higher reason why popes excommunicated kings, why the Church occupied ground, why medieval architects embattled church facades like city gates and ranged saints above a frieze of kings: to offer the imagination a palpable object in which to place the faith that could not be entrusted absolutely to princes.

The Church, however, is only a "center of the world" by courtesy of the allegorical reading of history:

> The true City of the saints is in heaven, though here on earth it produces citizens in whom it wanders as if in exile, waiting for the Kingdom of eternity.

> Cain became the father of Enoch, in whose name he founded a city—a city of the earth, not one traveling in exile through the world, but one contented with its own temporal peace and joy. (15. 1, 17)

Augustine's term for Christ's faithful here is *peregrinus*. Though this later meant "pilgrim," in the classical world it was simply a legal term, "alien," one whose god and whose primary civil allegiances and duties were not those of the city where he resided. Also it connoted "traveler," for to the ancients a *peregrinus* was simply someone away from home, his residence only a pause in a journey that would eventually return him to his native city.

Often Augustine describes the City of God, in its passage through time, as a *civitas peregrina*: not "pilgrim city" as it is sometimes improbably translated, but a community in exile, dwelling in the midst of the earthly city. When Augustine uses this image —rather than that of two separate, historically correlative city-states at war—he is more successful in rendering both the dynamics and the ambiguities of Christian religious experience.

For this view distinguishes the two cities according to their orientation in the dimension of time: while the City of Man determines citizenship by one's origins, the City of God derives it from the future, from one's living in hope of the kingdom of God. Augustine's millennial city is always beyond man's grasp, a reality he must reach for in faith, conceiving it through a time-oriented, figural imagination. It is the City of Man which attempts to achieve, *in time*, the unity and absolute fulfillment which only the absolute wisdom of God can achieve, outside of time's limit. In this way his message resembles that of the prophets: the city that seeks fulfillment within itself will disintegrate, as did the old Jerusalem, as did Babylon, as did Rome; the city which, though imprisoned within another city, maintains its faithful vision of a city elsewhere, a "center" beyond itself, the new Jerusalem, finds in that denial of self-sufficiency a source of unity and endurance. Thus the *civitas peregrina* realizes more adequately the time factor in Augustine's allegory—the present Church foreshadowed by the figures of the Old Testament, and itself a shadow of a full reality yet to come. Drawing on scriptural resources different from those that produced the symbol of Zion belligerent, it presents the people of God as a people in exodus, whose God requires no land, no city, no house, but may be worshiped in His transcendence anywhere. Also it evokes Christian associations of the "way" and the "following" of Christ.

Taken as a "moral" allegory, it presents the personal spiritual life not as a single dramatic reversal, the outcome of a climactic *psychomachia*, but as a continuous process, in which one's state of soul is measured both by what has gone before and by one's advance toward, or retreat from, a spiritual absolute. In the *Confessions* Augustine had rendered his own spiritual search as an exodus, from Tagaste to the unholy loves of Carthage, to the sophisters of Rome, and finally to a garden in Milan. In *The City of God* he says, "For us, Christ is the true road to follow; with Him as leader and savior, let us turn our steps away from the vain and hopeless cycles of the unbelievers" (12. 21). This is a significant contrast of Christ, the straight way, with the time-defeating concentric circles of pagan myth and cosmology.

When applied to the "allegorical" cities of historical institutions, this image allows us to realize better how two "cities" may be "completely interfused" in their existence in the here and now. Two different realities may indeed occupy the same physical space if their orientation in the fourth dimension is different. When he treats the temporal City of God as a homogeneous, sharply demarcated polity, he often approximates the ancient view of the city as a "center of the world," a holy place where man is liberated from the terrors of both profane space and profane time. When, on the other hand, he presents it as a spiritually defined community sharing the general life of the city where it lives, yet still distinct from it, he catches some of the characteristic ambiguity of the Christian life —its founder a man but not a man, a Jew and yet not a Jew, a messiah but not the expected messiah; its prototheologian and representative proselyte both Paul and Saul, Greek and Jew, and a scandal to both. Also this image speaks sometimes to the authentic presence of Christians in the secular world:

> The two cities, the heavenly and earthly, intermingled as they have been from the beginning and are to be until the end of time . . . alike make use of temporal goods, and both are equally afflicted by temporal ills. (18.54)

This catches some of that submission to the tragic condition of humanity, that bond with the timebound and the physical, which distinguished Christ's redemptive acts, and which the central tradition of his Church has insisted on—a tradition Augustine had difficulty accepting after his encounter with Manicheism and Platonism. A measure of that difficulty can be seen in the further, more disturbing implications of *civitas peregrina*.

Peregrinus is the Roman legal term denoting resident aliens within a city, individuals outside the city's cult and laws, who were administered by a special praetor. Their participation in the city's affairs was restricted both by its laws and by their prior obligations to the city of their allegiance. Cicero had defined their civic responsibilities simply in negatives:

> The duty of a *peregrinus* is to pursue nothing but his own business, never to pry into the lives of others, and under no circumstances to concern himself with the public affairs of his host country.[10]

Whereas the authors of the apostolic generation had addressed Christians who often were literally *peregrini* in Ephesus or in Rome, Augustine writes to an audience of Roman citizens, to people like himself, sufficiently incorporated into the Roman world to be dismayed by the sack of its ancient capital, the titular city of their commonwealth. Just as his book redefines the nature of *civitas*, it renews the Christians' title as *spiritual* peregrini, whose membership in the City of God limits their involvement in the earthly city, describing it, as Cicero had, largely in negatives.

Civitas terrena—earthly city—remains an irresolvably ambiguous term. On one hand it is the city of exclusively immediate concerns, the City of Self and of self-sufficiency; in such a city the Christian can be only a stranger and an enemy within the gates. On the other hand, it is the place of one's mortal life, of one's human loyalties. Nothing in *The City of God* summons Christians literally out of the city. Augustine understood the stake that Christians had in Roman civilization and in the cities which epitomized it. A religion of city dwellers since the time of the first evangelists, organized in metropolitan districts, cosmopolitan in membership, Christianity offered the urbanized Mediterranean world not a pastoral paradise, the woods and fields of Virgil's Arcadia, but a counter-city.[11] Nor does *The City of God* summon Christians to dereliction of their duties as human beings. The life of the saints is a communal life (19. 5); the image of the *civitas peregrina* suggests how a group of resident aliens, dispersed throughout the classes and occupations of a city, may develop a cohesiveness and sense of mutual support based on their common nationality. (Such a city may be truly "interfused with" another, as Augustine says.) Furthermore, this social responsibility is interlocked with the concerns of the larger community in which they live: "as mortal life is the same for all, there ought to be common cause between the two cities in what concerns that life" (19. 17). Since its own well-being is fostered by peace among its diverse membership and peace with nonmembers too, the City of God "makes use of" the peace—such as it is— provided by the civil state, and "fosters and actively pursues along with other human beings a common platform in regard to all that concerns the mortal nature of man." Augustine devotes book 19 to demonstrating that the virtues of Christianity—charity, justice, the pursuit of peace—are exactly those that promote the commonweal of all the earthly city. Indeed, he says, a city having only citizens of God would far surpass in secular harmony any other city. For in Augustine's mind peace depends on the harmonious order of diverse beings, and harmony among men depends on their recognition and pursuit of a common goal. Adverting to this contrast, earlier in the work, of Christian unity and pagan diversity, he argues that Christians' common dedication to the Heavenly City should not only bind them together as an ideal community, but provide a basis for civil agreement on the nature of such virtues as justice, humility, and mercy, which might foster the peace of the earthly city though they are pursued for the sake of the heavenly (19. 23–27).

Nevertheless, the *civitas terrena* and the *civitas peregrina* are two communities and as the latter is figurally linked to the City of God, so the former inevitably corresponds with the City of Mammon. Augustine cannot describe Christians as dual citizens, an image used by the Stoic Seneca.[12] They are *not* citizens of the earthly city, however they may make common cause with it. For him citizenship carried implications of spiritual allegiance and of religious cult. He reminds readers that Jeremiah urged the Jews to pray for Babylon, and that Saint Paul advised the Church to pray for kings and others in authority. But this is usually not enough for the earthly city, which insists on a cult of its own: "The heavenly City . . . has been unable to share with the earthly city a common religious legislation." Therefore his professions of common cause all are linked with qualifications—"so long as matters of faith and worship are not involved"—and usually suggest a restrained and passive presence for Christians in the earthly city:

> So long as her life in the earthly city is that of a captive and an alien . . . she has no hesitation about keeping in step with the civil law which governs matters pertaining to the sustenance of mortal life. (19. 17)

Christians "use" the civil peace and "comply" with state authority. They do not build the city, they do not reform its laws, they do not meddle in the public affairs of their host country.

The image of a "wayfaring" people allows Augustine to make imaginatively real the relationship between religious faith and temporal process—the way that the Church, and each of its members, may wax and wane in devotion to the following of Christ, and also the real presence of Christians in the tragic condition of human life in time ("It is our mortality we have in common"). But they are not present to that secular world in the same way that the citizens of man are. Their minds centered on a City Beyond, they perceive the coordinates of time differently from those for whom the present city is the only reality. For them, this city is only the Way; and in Augustine's mind, the City Beyond does not incorporate the Way and make it holy. He does not believe that man, sheltered in God, may make a home in this world. Nor is he able to imagine a civil order which would be religiously neutral. Etienne Gilson, commenting on *The City of God*, proposes a possible tertium quid, midway between the two symbolic cities—"a third city, which would be temporal like the earthly city, yet just in a temporal way, that is striving for a temporal justice obtainable by appropriate means." However, he points out, "such an idea seems never to have occurred to St. Augustine . . . not through any failure to foresee the beneficent influence that the City of God . . . can and ought to exercise on temporal societies; . . . rather, it was due to the close association between the two notions of *world* and of *evil*, so spontaneously linked together in his mind."[13]

Augustine had no intention of devaluing the long and ambiguous struggle of men to improve the quality of their lives. But such devaluation was a necessary consequence of his investing the historically present city with the symbolism of Babylon, that place of captivity, exile, and longing, while depicting Christ's faithful as an alien people whose eyes are turned from this city to a center in the infinite distance, a messianic Jerusalem at the end of time. For such a people, the present city is put "in perspective" and "out of focus." Its chronicle is written in another, and less significant, book.

In some measure this may be, as Gilson suggests, a blind spot in Augustine's imagination, stemming from his unconscious association of "world" and "evil." But it is also a recognition, by a man of considerable psychological subtlety, that the goals of human comfort and physical sufficiency cannot be achieved without a wholeminded absorption in them, a devotion which precludes devotion to God. The earthly city stays; the citizens of God sojourn. Augustine assumes that the earthly city will be dominated by those who have an exclusive interest in securing immediate advantages for man—that is, by egotists, though of varying degrees of enlightenment and philanthropy. The qualifications of Christian commitment to the earthly city, "so long as matters of faith and worship are not involved," do not refer so much to any traces of the old pagan municipal cults still lingering in the third decade of the fifth century, as to the Christian maxim that where a man's treasure is, there will be his heart also. Augustine was convinced that the short-term goods of man could not be attained without a commitment to attaining them which amounted to a religious conviction and that when they were attained, man would lose sight of God's absolute kingship over the world, and worship instead the human *civitas* which brought these blessings.

Historically speaking, however, this insight proved difficult to maintain. Augustine's collapsing of Roman ideals and Roman decadence into one *civitas terrena* did not resolve the question of the significance of human secular endeavor. Gilson observes that "the possibility of a unified temporal order, valid and justifiable in itself from the point of view of its proper end, did not suggest itself to St. Augustine."[14] This is not an oversight, but rather a consequence of the eschatological version of history. For the prophets, as we have seen, the laboring of the peoples comes to nothing, the toiling of the nations ends in fire. The image of history offered by the New Testament lacks even the Old Testament's sense of a theophanic revelation throughout time. The Christian scriptures begin with five detailed accounts of God's most personal self-revelation and intervention in history, through Christ and the Holy Spirit, but then discount all subsequent events in anticipation of Christ's promised return, depicted in the final book, Revelation, when the world of the past will end and time will be no more. Between these two climactic revelations hangs a slack of historical episodes purely profane in character (the poet W. H. Auden called it the Time Being[15]). Where the Son of Man is lifted up, where stands the throne of God and of the Lamb, there is Jerusalem; the rest is Rome. The "secular" world of history is confused with the "profane" world of figural insignificance.

So to call into question the reality and significance of historical events is to invite a schizophrenic view of the earthly city, in which secular deeds are not liable to religious interpretation, and yet the state is taken as an embodiment of spiritual principles and entrusted with millennarian hopes. To a secular imagination, especially one of imperial bias, Augustine's vision is subversive and divisive. To juggle temporal expediency and eschatological wisdom is unthinkable. One or the other must prevail. From Nero to Julian the empire had attempted to attack and destroy the competing city, to restore the cosmic unity of the City of Man. Augustine's image can deal easily with those struggles. But *The City of God* cannot acknowledge the contemporary empire's attempt to resolve the bicentric cosmos by assimilating the Church. The account of the Christian emperors in book 5 makes the point of distinguishing their lives as Christians from their duties as emperors. But in a world where holiness is the supreme value, any government must seek to make itself holy. When only the City of God is significant, then the state must wear the mask of the City of God. Nor did Augustine anticipate the extent to which the medieval church would indeed "occupy ground" and acquire a hierarchical and centralized administration very similar to the empire's. For the next millennium, and in some ways down to our own time, the evangelized world was to be vexed with a war not between flesh and spirit, or between pagan and Christian, but between lords civil and lords ecclesiastical, both believers, both acting in the name of God, both asserting the holiness of their administration, and both invoking Augustine's imagery of the two cities. Politically speaking, Augustine's dichotomy of sacred and secular was obsolete even as he wrote, for the Christianization of Rome and the Romanization of Christianity had advanced to the point that Augustine himself, as Bishop of Hippo, could invoke the "secular arm" to suppress a religio-political insurrection of Donatist peasants, and could die as leader of his besieged city when the pagan or heretical Vandals cornered in it the army of Bonifacius, Rome's somewhat uncertain arm in Africa.

Augustine's metaphor of two cities was soon to render the Church as a state, and the State as a church. After Constantine, the kingdom of God was translated from imagination to reality. As bishops became imperial officials and dressed as magistrates, the Christian church ceased to look like—or be—a residence, but was built in an adaptation of the *basilica*, a public hall used by the civil magistrate, who sat on a raised dais beneath a statue of the emperor (*basileus* in Greek). Such a building suited the magisterial bishop, who during religious ceremonies sat in state before the altar and, later, beneath an icon of the kingly God; and whose jurisdiction coincided with the secular *civitas* or urban region. The

Christianized empire was proclaimed the *Civitas Dei*, its alliance of Christian ruler with earthly Church taken as a symbolic reality, a prefiguring of Christ's kingdom on earth as foretold in the Apocalypse.

In the East, where Constantinople had been dedicated in a calculated meld of imperial and Christian symbols, the patriarchs of the Church had developed a theology almost indistinguishable from that of the ancient city-cults. The *basileus* in his city not only corresponded to God in heaven as center and regulator, but actually served to link the city with heaven, as a mediator through whom spiritual power flowed into the social order, so that the emperor transcended the distinction made between priest and king. At the Milvian Bridge the Christian God Himself had chosen Constantine, the city's founder, as emperor of the earth; therefore, the emperors of Byzantium might call their city the New Jerusalem, and seek to make it as rich as that city in Revelation, and call their empire *oekumene*, the universe.[16] In the West, after a hiatus of almost four hundred years, Charlemagne devised his own Christendom, a unifocal secular kingdom dedicated to, and enjoying the protection of, the divine Christ. *The City of God*, we are told, was his bedside book.

> Temporal ruler of the nations which it was his care to lead to God under the aegis of the Church, Charles might have thought that he had brought the mystical city upon earth to embody it in an empire: the body would be the empire; the soul, the mystical city. Why would the Emperor have found delight in such a book as *The City of God*, were it not because the empire which he himself had built was the embodiment of the City of God?[17]

Necessary to such an empire was an exalted vision of its earthly head, though not so celestial as Constantine's. Charlemagne too thought to draw on both Rome and Jerusalem for its symbolism, presenting himself both as Augustus Caesar and as *Christus Domini*, the annointed of the Lord, who both supervised the Church's hierarchy and enforced their religion on his subjects; and he devised a system of ceremonial, ritual, and theology which attracted to his kingship the ancient aura of divinity, accommodated to Christianity by his professed submission to God as absentee liege-lord.

In effect, Charlemagne and the Byzantine emperors resolved

Augustine's tension of sacred and secular, seeking to perpetuate, in a Christian form, the ancient myth of divine kingship. Nowhere is this more evident than in the design of churches, which became symbolic cities in order to represent the imperial power. To enact the idea of "the kingdom of God," post-Constantinian churches appropriated some of the emblems of the divine emperor, such as his formal entry into a city—*parousia* or *epiphany*—through a triumphal arch, and his enthronement beneath a hemisphere symbolizing the cosmos; these emblems became the liturgical processions, the towered facade, and the altar baldachin of the Christian church.[18] Whatever survived of the old Roman *imperium* was still symbolized by the *civitas*; framing the emperor's churches as cities promoted that confusion of secular sway and religious mandate which Virgil had once given Rome.

In the East, the confusion of the two cities was absolute. Eusebius, the bishop of Caesarea who initiated the imperial theology of the Byzantine state, included in his *Ecclesiastical History* an address he gave at the dedication of a new church in Tyre.[19] The earliest written account of Christian church architecture and furnishings, it offers with that description an explanation of the church's spiritual significance. Eusebius begins by quoting Psalm 87 on the City of God. With this scriptural prototype as foundation, he can develop allegorical parallels between the physical and the congregational "church," and between the building's structural arrangement and the progress of the single soul to salvation. He conceives the church as a linear succession of spaces, leading the visitor from an imposing gateway, which he associates with the praise of "God, the universal King," down a triumphal way to a golden throne room where the Eucharist is celebrated. Later, as a distinctive Byzantine architecture took form, it was natural for it to symbolize, with its dome above a square, the perfection of the heavenly city come down upon the earth. The Byzantine liturgy had a role for the emperor as earthly equivalent of Christ, and the church itself was conceived as an imperial throne room for him and for the God whose viceroy he was. To advance through its gates and toward the dome, as to enter Constantinople at the Golden Gate and walk up the *Mesê* toward the Imperial Palace, was to come into the City of God and move down a triumphal way into the enthroned presence of the Universal King.

In the West the identification of the two powers was never

complete, and so the symbolism was more complex. Charlemagne had his counterparts of Eusebius, a "palace clergy" drawn from the royal family and the nobility, and dedicated to a principle of theocratic absolutism. Lacking cities and churches of the splendor of Byzantium, he created a group of royal abbeys each made to resemble a fortified city, not only because it might serve frequently as his palace, but also because it symbolized his divine right to rule this earthly *civitas*, including the Church temporal. As the abbey was a figure of the heavenly city, so the emperor's power on earth was a figure of Christ's in heaven. One of those abbeys, St.-Denis, later became the shrine and symbol of the Capetian monarchy; where, Saint Bernard said, the things which were Caesar's were indeed rendered unto Caesar, but where were not delivered with equal fidelity to God the things that were God's. Rebuilt in the mid-twelfth century by its abbot Suger (who had once been regent of France), and reconsecrated with a ceremony in which King Louis VII enacted a Christological role, its towered and embattled facade and its great windows, whose stained glass suggested the jewelled walls of the New Jerusalem, became the prototype of the "gothic" churches of the High Middle Ages.[20]

However, the western Church was by no means so subservient to the power of kings as was the Byzantine patriarchate. In the view of its partisans, it was not the emperor who had inherited Caesar's power to dispose of all things on earth, but rather the bishops and the Bishop of Rome. Part of the papal struggle against the emperors in the late twelfth and early thirteenth centuries involved the transferring of such urban and kingly symbolism from the royal majesty to Christ as the *Majestas Domini*. Doubtless to many ecclesiastics their own majesty, rather than Christ's, was the essence of the struggle. But they, like Augustine, asserted the Church as a counterkingdom, here and now, reclaiming men from absolute submission to Caesar. So whether the adversary was Satan, or only Frederick II, Christian church architecture was for a thousand years cast in the form of a stylized and miniaturized fortress city— Christ's dour comments on ecclesial monumentalism (Mk. 13:1–2) notwithstanding. The orb atop St. Peter's dome proclaims the Church's power over *urbs* and *orbis*; the towers of Notre Dame de Paris, with rows of kings below, assert the absolute kingship of God and the endurance of His city against all assaults, from the emperor's *palatium* to the gates of hell. So the figural mind assimilated into spiritual significance the chief internal political struggle of medieval Christendom.

The same imaginative power developed the *civitas peregrina*, Augustine's symbol of a detached and timebound Christianity, into an experienced reality. For the heavenly Jerusalem, as a goal, might have its counterparts by way of allegory. It was crucial to the development of Judaism and of Christianity that for many centuries even the earthly Holy City should have been hard to reach or inaccessible. The rituals of Judaism for nearly 2000 years have been rituals of the diaspora, performed in a lack of the holy places. Medieval Christendom based its three great symbols, crusade, pilgrimage, and cathedral, on the difficulty of access to Jerusalem.

Traveling to the Holy City from Christian Europe had been difficult enough since Constantine's time; his mother, Helena, may have been the first Christian to make the journey there a devotional and expiatory act. As a consequence of her visit, the True Cross was found there, and a number of basilicas built to contain and honor the holy places associated with Christ's death. At the end of the fourth century, when Saint Jerome went there to spend the last half of his life translating the Bible, he found Jerusalem a cosmopolis of pilgrims. Through the Dark Ages, even after Jerusalem fell into Moslem hands in 638, the arduous journey east stood as the ultimate measure of Christian devotion. The posthumous sanctification of Charlemagne required inventing his journey to Palestine, from which he had returned with the relics of the crucifixion.

When Jerusalem was taken by the Seljuks in 1070, Christian pilgrims were harassed, robbed, and enslaved. Pilgrimage soon became crusade. The removal of the Holy City *outside* "Christendom," and the hazards of war now added to those of travel, preoccupied Pope Urban II in his speech at the Council of Clermont proclaiming the First Crusade. After reciting some Moslem atrocities, and reminding the French of their tradition of valor, he offered the bishops a holy war that would redeem Jerusalem to Christian rule, relieve Byzantium, and give vent to the internal warfare of overcrowded Europe. Whatever social, political and ecumenical realities his crusade may have served, however, his speech refers not to the real Jerusalem but to the figural:

> Let therefore hatred depart from among you, let your quarrels end, let wars cease, and let all dissensions and controver-

sies slumber. Enter upon the road to the Holy Sepulchre; wrest that land from the wicked race, and subject it to yourselves. That land which as the Scripture says "floweth with milk and honey," was given by God into the power of the children of Israel. Jerusalem is the centre of the earth; the land is fruitful above all others, like another paradise of delights. This the Redeemer of mankind has made illustrious by His advent, has beautified by His residence, has consecrated by His passion, has redeemed by His death, has glorified by His burial.

This royal city, however, situated at the centre of the earth, is now held captive by the enemies of Christ, and is subjected by those who do not know God, to the worship of the heathens. She seeks therefore and desires to be liberated and does not cease to implore you to come to her aid. . . . Accordingly undertake this journey for the remission of your sins, with the assurance of the imperishable glory of the kingdom of heaven.[21]

The Pope's words evoke a complex of associations. First there is Jerusalem as the cosmological *axis mundi*, "center of the earth" and earthly paradise; the crusade becomes a mythic return to unity, a recovery and feudalizing of Paradise.[22] Then he evokes a series of scriptural images: the Old Testament promised land, goal of that ancient holy invasion, the exodus; a Gospel land, scene of Christ's life; and the Jerusalem enslaved of Saint Paul's letter to the Galatians. Finally the city is the messianic city of God, which Revelation had snatched away to the end of time, now restored within the reach of man, beyond a more manageable boundary in space, though still a city far off, a deferred vision. Urban seeks to create in his pilgrimage-crusade a model of Augustine's *civitas peregrina*, a disciplined body drawn from all classes and nations, an armed column on the march toward Jerusalem, a devoted people withdrawn from secular and selfish struggle, for the service of God.

The success of that First Crusade, of course, gave Jerusalem only brief deliverance; and so the crusade proved to be one of the enduring spiritual, political, and social realities of the Middle Ages. In the same epoch, a new religious architecture developed in Europe, founded on a complex allegorical imagination which was capable of sustaining not only the historical Jerusalem and the eschatological New Jerusalem, but also a symbolic analogue present in time and more accessible in space. The geographical inaccessibility of Jerusalem created not only a multitude of other pilgrimage centers in Europe, but an architecture and iconography which symbolized both the City and the Way.

Pilgrimages to Rome, originally to the shrine of Peter's relics, as early as the fourth century assumed the form of visits to a succession of basilicas corresponding to the "stations" of Christ's life and to the holy places in Palestine. In the Renaissance, Pope Sixtus V developed a street plan for Rome based on the pilgrimage routes, with broad straight avenues providing both uncongested access and a view, from a distance, of the pilgrim's goal. Many of the cathedrals built in Italy and France during the eleventh and twelfth centuries, contemporary with the crusades, had inlaid in their floors a labyrinth, its center called "Jerusalem," its purpose evidently a penitential journey, made on one's knees, to that mystic center.[23]

And so the church building became the figure of Jerusalem. As symbol of the heavenly city, it united the finite and mortal with the infinite and perfect, the body with the soul, natural with supernatural, man with God. Like the Jerusalem in Revelation, the church represented a perfectly harmonious form, its architecture revealing the same fascination with a mathematically inclusive cosmos based on symbolic numbers—3, 4, 7, and 12—and on symbolic geometrical figures, notably the hexagon and octagon.[24] As the visionary Jerusalems of Ezekiel and John had twelve gates, three on each side, so the churches came to present three doors on each front (except the apse)—even when, as at Chartres, the three had no relation to the tripartite interior structure of nave and aisles. And as in those apocalyptic cities each gate was associated with a tribe of Israel or an Apostle, so these doors were associated with the figures of salvation history, and decorated with their statues. Oriented to the four quarters of the world, the church's four faces acquired allegorical significance, partly derived from scripture but also indebted to a solar mythos. The church's nave, and the congregation within it, faced east toward the coming of light, the entrance of God; north and south were contrasted as shadow and light, Old Testament and New, spiritual alienation versus the light and fire of the Holy Spirit. The west, or the chief gate for mortal men, became a battleground of darkness and light, of demons and the angelic forces of the City of God, struggling for the human soul: the dangerous point where one crossed from the secular world to the sacred.[25]

The church's interior is part of its religious significance as well. The modern German architect Rudolf Schwarz, in a meditation on religious architecture, experiences the church's encompassing wall as the symbol of spiritual harmony:

> Within this center everything is present once more in transformed form. The universe is at one in the innermost spot. This, then, is center: the common heart, the going out and the coming home of all things, that infinite within out of which life is lived and to which it returns. Here is the "hidden shrine" of the universe. And hence it is that to enter into the center means to go into the whole, into the undivided, into the unbroken.[26]

The indifference of medieval people to the exteriors of their churches, which modern planners have sought to remedy by demolishing other buildings that interfere with the perspective, issued from their thinking of the church as interior space, which was entered through a passage narrow and difficult, an experience kinetic and tactile rather than strictly visual. Once through the gates, the Christian worshiper entered the center of the world, a concentric city, unified space arranged progressively from the laity in the nave to clergy in the chancel and the celebrant priest before the altar, where the power of God came down on men.

Abbot Suger, that articulate twelfth-century cleric whose renovation of St.-Denis is taken to be the prototype of the Gothic, explains that to enter the church building should be to experience, "anagogically," one's entrance into the heavenly Jerusalem. As a secular man, the associate of kings, he was fascinated by rich and splendid things; as a medieval Christian, Augustine's heir, he inhabited a world made manifold by the creative word of God. In all the liturgical arts he patronized, he sought to realize in material things the symbols he knew in words, the words of scripture. He wished to create a shrine whose magnificence would not only honor the saints and the entire Church, but would, by its contrast with the workaday world outside, remind visitors of the difference between the things of earth and the glory hereafter. So he sought, in his new church, to rival the splendor of Constantinople's Hagia Sophia and

Jerusalem's Temple of Solomon, descriptions of which he had read or heard from pilgrims and crusaders.

The old abbey church had been, appropriately to its purpose, a closed container for the monks' choir and the crypt of relics, shrines within a shrine. The sense of Suger's alterations was to throw the church open, to make it a passage rather than a receptacle. Replacing a single constricted entrance, he built a new western front with three wide doors corresponding to the aisles within the church; he lengthened the nave and cleared it of transverse obstructions; and in place of the shallow hemispherical apse behind the altar—a cul-de-sac containing the reliquaries—he built a long choir in which a continuous double passage, or ambulatory, looped around the relics now elevated for display. In his new church a stream of pilgrims might enter one portal, move up an aisle, pass around the ambulatory, and exit down the opposite aisle. The church's community was now not a cloister of men vowed to one place for life, but a multitude in passage. The new building was meant to enhance the visual and kinetic experience of pilgrims, not to contain the voices of communal prayer. Mass and eucharist, as rite and *sacramentum* of an inclosed group, become proportionally less significant in a church structured for the continuous initiation of strangers. The genius of Gothic architecture was to actualize in its interior the symbolic possibilities of light, restoring actual experience to a spiritual figure. To pass through the doors of the church was to pass from the light of common day to the enhanced, dramatized, and polychrome light within; morally, it was to pass (as Suger's inscriptions said) from confusion to truth; anagogically it was to pass from earth to heaven. Many of the sculptured tympanums over the cathedrals' doors portray Christ sitting in judgment before the gates of the heavenly city. The City of God, says the tympanum, lies not beyond these doors, but beyond the limit of time, encompassed only by the wisdom of God. Yet the living man who enters here may experience, if he has the imagination for it, what it means to pass from profane to sacred, from self to love, from Satan to Christ, from the City of Man to the City of God.

In his meditation on the symbolism of various church designs, Rudolph Schwarz calls the Gothic the plan of "sacred journey." Whereas the enclosed, circular shrine is appropriate for a people who find God intimately in their midst, for whom the shrine is cosmos enough, this elongated form, with a promise of light at its end, is appropriate for "the community which comes into being when the shared center of love flees into the infinite. . . . As long as all eyes cling to the distant light and as long as the light shines into each heart illuminating it inwardly, this form, too, remains a form of communion. The light binds the human beings together."[27] The cathedral, then, is like the messianic Jerusalem created by the prophets. It symbolizes a spiritual center which in actuality lies "beyond" the community which finds unity in it. It rests in the shared imagination of a people conscious of their orientation in time and illuminated by their faith in the word of God. To enter the church in that spirit is to be reminded that one is on the Way to another City.

The linear movement of the Romanesque or Gothic church corresponds to its people's linear movement, in time, toward God; it was meant to be experienced in motion—approached from a distance (hence the siting often on high ground, as at Chartres and at Durham, a city on a hill), entered in a sudden transformation of experience, walked through from porch to altar. Its space is dynamic and relative, not absolute. Schwarz continues:

> In the earlier [circular] plans the inner space . . . corresponded to the structure of the universe. . . . Here it is not so simple. The way-form has no real, continuing space. Its net-like structure interlaces a world which is travelled and yet not experienced, which completely loses itself in the uncertain. The inner "locating" in the way-form provides only a "relative space." . . . The comparative space of the network is transparent to the space of the universe.[28]

A world traveled but not experienced: the image of pilgrims en route to their heavenly city, a kinetic image sensitive to time, also conveys something significant about the quality of the Christian's participation in the life and action of the historical world, the earthly city, through which he is passing. For the early Church fathers, history collapsed into a Time Being between Christ's first and second comings. Schwarz discovers in architecture a comparable evacuation of meaning from the secular world:

> They have no home. The form makes them fugitive on the earth, it consumes them in representing an endless process of

consummation. The earth is but the material which bears their train, it is not a staked claim. This folk founds no cities, cultivates no countryside. The things which other peoples take so for granted—that man, sheltered in God, also has a home in the world, that wherever there is sacred form, a reverent delimitation occurs, and that the building of a church means primarily the enclosure of a piece of the world which has now become as God originally intended it to be—all these ideas are foreign to this people.[29]

This is not, of course, a description of the culture of the High Middle Ages, but rather an extreme statement of the implications of a figural imagination in which all reality is conceived as Way, in which God's people is a "remnant" that lives exiled in Babylon. Evacuating the temporal or secular world of symbolic significance, save that of antagonist or of shadowy prefiguration, it symbolizes true Christian detachment; but it invites unholy powers to fill that vacuum with a symbolism of their own. Man cannot regard neutrally his most manifold artifact, the city. The imagination shapes and interprets experience. The city we experience, the city in secular history, demands imaginative interpretation. When the heavenly city lies too far away, and the figural imagination wanes in intensity, the City of Man—egotism in its every political and moral form—rises up, in the splendor of Jerusalem.

3: The Triumph of the Map

> *The paper is whiter*
> *For these black lines.*
> *It glares beneath the webs*
> *Of wire, the designs of ink,*
> *The planes that ought to have genius,*
> *The volumes like marble ruins*
> *Outlined and having alphabetical*
> *Notations and footnotes.*
> *The paper is whiter.*
> *The men have no shadows*
> *And the women have only one side.*

> Wallace Stevens, "The Common Life"

SATAN, NO NOVICE TEMPTER, PUT JESUS' TEMPTATIONS UNDER his feet and bade him *look*, hoping that physical eminence and visual control would generate a will to domination. Stones, temples, kingdoms of the world—adroitly he increases the scope and exaltation of the eye. Jesus, of course, neutralizes each prospect with a saying. Men who build the kingdoms and cities of the world, however, have rarely resisted providing themselves with the symbols of visual control, to complement their political power.

Naturally visual control and social order are related. Where order is preserved by armed force, the advantages of superior elevation are several and obvious. In Aristotle's more benignant *polis*, just government as well as defense depend on the citizens' visual comprehension of their city. The city must be *eusynoptos*, capable of being taken in at a single view. This not only facilitates signaling among the defenders, but gives the citizens a sense of being comprehended within a single body (*Politics* 7. 4–5). Kevin Lynch's influential study *The Image of the City* has suggested that the residents of modern cities can more adequately participate in urban life when the physical city has "legibility"—when its parts are easily recognized and can be organized by the imagination into coherent patterns.[1] Yet in the long history of urban planning there persist certain forms of visual arrangement in which such practical and communitarian motives yield to assertions of a central authority whose secular power is draped in religious devices.

The foursquare holy city surmounted by its shrine; the church facade embattled like a city; the straight way to the immortal Jerusalem: these were the architectural motifs, considered earlier in this book, that clothed a group of religious ideals in the reality of the imagination. Usually the symbolic quality of this city was made apparent in the disparity between it and the actual historical city. This pairing of the actual with the symbolic invites man to conceive realities beyond himself and beyond his present circumstances. The image of the holy city, in its verbal or iconic form, summons man into faith.

The same imaginative process that gave reality to "Jerusalem" and its ideals often called into question the reality of the secular city, reducing or denying its significance, transferring absolute power from it to a city at the end of time. The princes of the City of Man, of course, have been little content with such diminishment. Again and again they have sought to realize those symbolic images in their own cities. Repudiating the power of the imagination, they have striven to create a city where spiritual realities are brought on the stage, here and now, as altogether physical attributes of the rule of the prince.

"Brought on the stage": drama is born of the desire to translate verbal symbols into spectacle, to manifest the inward vision, to make the imaginary real. Furthermore, it is a social art, it is the art of the city. As the city's princes (aristocratic or plutocratic) have long patronized and sustained the theater, so the arts of theatrical spectacle have sustained and complimented the prince, enacting for him otherwise imaginary pretensions to religious sanction for his power. The king is not simply "the principal ruffian," as Thomas Paine once said, but rather a role (like the other city roles, outlasting most of its incumbents), sustained by ritual, ceremonial, and spectacle, arts borrowed from drama and from the theatrical aspects of religion. Ascending the ziggurat in the center of the cosmological city, the king enacts a role as man aspiring to the wisdom, immortality, and perfection of the gods. Copulating with the priestess he is the sky god bringing fertility to earth. Ordering the city in its laws, its citizens, and its buildings he is the creator god bringing dynamic form into the midst of chaos. As he enacts these roles, he assumes to himself the awesomeness of the figure he represents. And the city becomes his scene, the complementary backdrop for his acts. Machiavelli observed that a prince is wiser to trust in the loyalty of his people than in the strength of his citadels. But the citadel, in a variety of forms, becomes often a dramatic realization of the prince's power. *Palatium* is at once the emperor's residence, his suzerainty, and the divine origins of his power.[2] The king's power is secured as the people see it enacted, and the king finds his power confirmed in his ability to oversee his city.

Overt religious symbology, since the Renaissance, has been restricted to church architecture. Nevertheless it has continued to influence urban design. Indeed, since the Renaissance it has flourished as never before, in unacknowledged and thus corrupted forms, inviting men to worship a divinity at hand—the prince, the state, or even the power of democratic man. In each case, the divinity imposes on its worshipers the architectural equivalent of some magical form, running its geometric scheme through the less perfect configurations of common life, asserting visual patterns of order and control over the more intangible forms of word and memory. Emphasizing the visual and the aesthetic, this architecture suppresses its victims' sense of the fourth and even the third dimensions of their experience: in place of historical and eschatological consciousness, it offers the illusion of space detached from time.

An Egyptian hieroglyph for the city was a circle enclosing a cross. Emblem of the city's wall and crossroads, it also portrays the metaphysical city of community and exchange or the religious city whose magic circle wards off demons and whose quadratic axis allows man to aspire to a place among the gods. But it also conveys the city's darker side, its wall for confinement or exclusion, its military parade routes converging on the palace of the god-king. Actual cities in the ancient world, of course, seldom attained any such geometric perfection, but rather rose in irregular clusters reflecting their topography, customs, and gradual growth. The processional ways of Uruk, Jerusalem, Rome, and Byzantium must have made their point not so much by the regular shape they gave the city's plan, but by the visual and kinesthetic pomp of the military and religious processions they channeled, and by the splendor of the walls and gates through which they passed. The power of the ancient city was dramatized primarily by forms of magnificence that rose vertically before an observer on the ground.

Walls and gates, at once military necessities and magical religious devices, were attributes of kingship, and the king took a personal ceremonial role in siting and erecting them.[3] The Prologue to *Gilgamesh* invites us to admire the works of that king:

> In Uruk he built walls, a great rampart,
> and the temple of blessed Eanna
> for the god of the firmament Anu, and for
> Ishtar the goddess of love.
> Look at it still today: the outer
> wall where the cornice runs,
> it shines with the brilliance of copper;
> and the inner wall, it has no equal.
> Touch the threshold, it is ancient. . . .
> Climb upon the wall of Uruk; walk along it, I say;
> regard the foundation terrace and
> examine the masonry: is it not
> burnt brick and good?
> The seven sages laid the foundations.[4]

This view of the haughty walls of Uruk introduces the poem's fundamental theme, the pride of Gilgamesh, invincible in arms, overweening among his subjects.

Plutarch's account of the founding of Rome, however fabulous in its particulars, can be taken seriously as an account of the king's role in uniting military and religious motives in the founding of a city. Having prevailed by fraud over his brother Remus, Romulus chose a site called Roma Quadrata, foursquare Rome, designated by his augurs; dug a pit at its center, offered sacrifice, buried in it the victims; called the spot *mundus* (the cosmos); yoked a cow and a bull to a brazen ploughshare and traced in the soil the city's perimeter, at intervals interrupting the furrow to provide a gate.

These intervals do not represent merely a planner's forethought as to where openings should be placed in the wall when it was built. They were immediately necessary, to allow access to the camp without defiling that sacred boundary. When Remus stepped across that furrow—unceremoniously, contemptuously—Romulus killed him.⁵ Once sketched upon the earth, a strongman's design at once can attain such holiness that to cross it is both sacrilege and lese majesty.

The founding of Constantinople, which is better attested historically, involved the same emphasis on a sacred periphery, the same blend of military and religious motives, the same ceremonial function for the king. Having chosen an excellently defensible site, Constantine inaugurated his new capital with an elaborate theatrical in which he acted the role of a Christian Romulus:

> When he went to mark out the circuit of the city, he walked round it with a spear in his hand; and . . . when his attendants thought that he was measuring out too large a space, one of them came up to him and asked him, "How far, O prince?" and . . . the emperor answered, "Until he who goes before me comes to a stop"; by this answer clearly manifesting that some heavenly power was leading him on.⁶

At the city's dedication, a reliquary statue was set up in the Forum of Constantine, the city's largest, adjacent to the palaces; it was a statue of Apollo with its head changed to Constantine's and encircled with sunrays made of the nails from Christ's cross. Inside was a relic from that cross.⁷ Thus Constantine became the first of a series of upstart kings deliberately using the Roman mode as a legitimizing theatrical, melding it with the iconography of Christianity, and directing attention to a king at the city's center, who orders and illuminates his realm as the sun god does the cosmos.

Although Constantinople had a processional way, the Mesê, joining all its major fora as it advanced from the grandiose Golden Gate to the city's innermost shrines and palaces, the city itself was not laid out on a geometric model. And Rome, however *quadrata* in mythical origin, was destined by its hilly topography to labyrinthine irregularity. Hence, for such cities, the emphasis on walls and gates as visible synechdoches for magical enclosure; hence the setting up, within the city, of symbolic gateways in the form of triumphal arches. Doubtless this reverence reflects the gate's military vulnerability, but the gate seems also to have symbolized the translation from ordinary reality into perfection. Related to both is the ancient association of the gate with the royal power. The king's judgment seat was at the city gate. There his *parousia*, his triumphal entry, began. It was in combat at a rival city's gates that commemorative stelae would depict him. The iconography of the High Middle Ages, so asserting the kingship of Christ, depicted him seated in judgment above the church's door, and bore his image or his transubstantiated body in royal procession, and showed him triumphant over death at the shattered gates of hell. Shakespeare, with his imaginative sympathy for the classical and medieval past, accurately dramatized Caius Marcius winning his cognomen, and all but kingship, in a heroic single-handed sally into the gates of Corioli (*Coriolanus* 1. 5), and Henry V disproving his reputation as a wastrel by breaching the walls of Harfleur and entering its gates in triumph (*Henry V* 3. 1, 3).

This is not to say that the pre-Renaissance world was so fascinated with the vertical forms of magnificence that it attached no significance to the city's ground plan, either ideal or actual. But the symbolic plan of the ancient city, as a model of the foursquare cosmos, was usually experienced in imagination and in ritual rather than by actual inspection. Girt by its powerful wall and sacred gates, holding at its heart an isomorphic model of the cosmos' perfect geometric form, the actual city could arrange itself—for better or for worse—according to less rigid social, economic, topographic, and personal schemata. Though kings might erect new buildings and open longer and broader processional ways, it would require both new technology and a new visual imagination before that ideal geometric form could be imposed on the physical and spiritual fabric of the actual city.

Of course the will to impose such form was not unknown to the ancient world. The Roman new towns, colonies or permanent army camps, originated with a symmetrical design. Beginning on a clear and level site, and working for defined and limited purposes, military engineers could trace, as on a tablet, a rectangular limit transversed by two intersecting avenues, and gridded into sites for each cohort of the legion, or for each quarter of the new town. Their design would unite military convenience with the dictates of a cosmological religion.[8] The Roman architectural writer Vitruvius, who had himself been a military engineer, began his treatise on the siting of cities with abundantly practical considerations of topography and local climate, but found himself unable to resist symbolical and magical factors in his design. Of course he starts with the walls and gates. Then taking up the internal arrangement of streets, he first advises that they be designed to ventilate the city while baffling unhealthy winds. At once, however, he declares that there are exactly eight winds, one from each quarter of the sky and one midway between each two quarters, and that streets should be aligned in a radiocentric style in between these eight points on the city's circular perimeter. He then turns to geometrical schemes for laying out such an octangular city. The geometer's rule and dividers replace the tangible experience of the mistral, the tramontane, or the levanter. Convenience in social intercourse yields to aesthetic and religious considerations of harmony, regularity, and perfect inclosure.[9]

The rediscovery of Vitruvius in the Renaissance accompanied the birth of a technology and a visual imagination that would jointly make possible the realization of magico-religious symbols in the physical shape and life of the city, as an enactment of the power of the new secular prince. Vitruvius had classified architectural representations into three: ichnographic (ground plan), orthographic (elevation), and scaenographic (perspective). In the Middle Ages and in the early Renaissance, representations of cities were invariably either orthographic or clumsy attempts at the scaenographic. They depicted the city as it might be seen by an observer outside the city, perhaps situated on an actual or imagined eminence nearby. In the Renaissance, a less directly experiental order, corresponding to the ichnographic, began to dominate the depiction of the city. A measure of this new order is the cult of the plan, both actual and ideal. And the techniques of perspective, when perfected, were pressed into royal service, to make of the city's center a stage for the aestheticized acts of the king. Methods for rendering the city on paper soon were adapted to architectural forms, producing a Euclidean city, lacking any sense of the dimensions in which human life is cast.

Influenced by Vitruvius, the earliest Italian planners began a vogue for designing paper cities with compass, protractor, and ruler, sometimes against a background of numerology or astrology. Their geometric constructions, laid out like a compass rose, secularized the formerly religious motive to manifest not the power and perfection of the gods of heaven but (in its utopian version, the *città ideale*) the power of an idea, the ideal of the harmonious state; or (in its practical form, the city of the prince) the power of one man to shape his people's destinies and to command their service.

> The ideal city was, in fact, an artistic and political invention of its time, since it was founded on the principle that the perfect architectural and urban form of the city corresponded to the perfection of its political and social arrangements, conceived and carried out by the wisdom of the prince in the same way that the geometry of the plan and the beauty of the buildings were conceived and carried out by the skill of the architect.[10]

These designs, like all Renaissance works of art, were dedicated to princely patrons. Filarete designed an ideal city, Sforzinda, dedicated to Francesco Sforza, condottiere and duke of Milan. It is a Vitruvian octagram centering on a piazza with a palace at one end and a church at the other, while from each angle of the wall streets and canals converge there. Di Giorgio experimented with octagrams, hexagrams, and squares, laying out the streets in circles, grids, or spirals, but always with a great square at the center. His works were dedicated to his patron the Duc d'Urbino. These plans were graphics, executed in two dimensions, and they referred to real cities in the same way that Michelangelo's funerary sculpture refers to the Medicis.

Contemporary maps reveal that actual sixteenth-century cities were still medieval in character—a labyrinth within, a wall without. But in those cities were both the psychological pressure to actualize a geometric ideal, and rudiments of the political and technological power needed to do so. The geometric city began to move off paper and onto the earth. The most perfect examples are small star-shaped cities like Palmanova in Italy and Naarden in the Netherlands, built on cleared and level ground, the geographic equivalent of paper, where no previous construction or topographical irregularity might mar the grand design.

In these outpost cities the founding kings were motivated less by vanity than by military necessity. Gunpowder turned the *città ideale* into the new citadel. The city countered gunpowder and metal shot with oblique surfaces to deflect the enemy's missiles, and mounted its own artillery on projecting angles from which they could sweep the exterior base of the wall. The polygonal or star-shaped perimeter was ideal for both purposes. Radial avenues, running straight from a central *place d'armes* to the gates, aided the efficient deployment of the city's garrison and munitions. Jacques Perret, an architect who wrote his *Fortifications and Strategems* for Henri IV at the end of the sixteenth century, noted that cannon placed in the central square would command all approaches—a fact as useful in crowd control within the city as in war against forces from without.[11] His contemporary Andrea Palladio, in his *Four Books of Architecture*, advised his patrons, the noblemen of Vicenza:

> The principal streets, which we have called military, in the cities ought to be so comparted, that they may be straight, and lead from the gates of the city in a direct line to the greatest and principal piazza. . . . The palace of the prince, or of the signory (as it happens either to be a principality or a republic) ought to be joined thereto, so ought the mint, the public treasury, and the prisons.[12]

Palladio's "military" streets have an evident tactical purpose. But he is describing not an outpost, but a capital. The dramatic placement of the palace at the city's center, with the symbols of judiciary and fiscal power supporting it, is designed more for the psychological than the military support of the state. Palladio and Perret, and the other designers of that age, were interested in architectural means for securing the allegiance of the prince's subjects, which Machiavelli had said was more important than the fortress itself. A radiocentric plan channels energy both centrifugally and centripetally: the centrifugal forces are military and practical, the centripetal aesthetic and psychological.

The art theme of the *città ideale* was not restricted to the manufacture of polygonal ground plans and treatises on the analogy of geometrical and civil harmony. It was also the subject for scaenographic representation, that is, exercises in rendering perspective. Piero della Francesca's *La Città Ideale*, for example, presents the central square of such a city. It is ringed with three- and four-story buildings whose colonnades, window lines, and cornices are radii of a vanishing point in the painting's center. That point is concealed behind a large circular temple which fills much of the square. The viewer is made to feel that he stands at the central, most favored point in the composition, with the elements of the composition disposed before him in perfect bilateral symmetry. Significantly, della Francesca's ideal city is unpopulated: what mortal man would dare intrude his own oblique ways on that march of radials into infinity?

A king, perhaps, who would treat this city as his backdrop, a scene in the theatrical sense. The centripetal radials of perspective, like those of the military streets, helped dramatize the king's importance. In most Renaissance perspective studies, as in della Francesca's painting, the converging horizontals of the street's facades are terminated by another building set at right angles to the rest of the composition. The Venetian Sebastiano Serlio frankly presented these elements as theater sets. He used a medieval street as his comic stage, but chose classical architecture for the tragic, the mode which Aristotle had said presented men better than in real life. The classical theater had used as backdrop the *skene*, a building housing stage properties but treated in the tragedy as a royal palace. The Renaissance theater restored this convention by using as backdrop a palace with a central "royal door" and a balcony above.[13] Palladio designed the stage set for his Teatro Olimpico at Vicenza as a palace front flanked by avenues which, through a manipulation of perspective, seem to recede far into the distance. Like della Francesca's painting, it is an effect which suggests to the viewer that he occupies the optimum viewpoint, that he is at the center.

Of course kingship had always been theatrical. Pliny the Younger, writing a panegyric for Trajan, expressed the hope that his administration would be marked by *real* triumphs, rather than ones celebrating fictitious victories and employing chariots and actors borrowed from the theaters.[14] The Renaissance, however, came to think of the stage and the world as isomorphically linked, microcosm and macrocosm, as the ancient world had thought of the temple and the universe. And kings were the proper centers of attention in both. When Shakespeare launches *Henry V* with a prologue that wishes for a macrotheater—"a kingdom for a stage, princes to act / And monarchs to behold the swelling scene!"—he acknowledges the hyperbole involved in daring to "cram / Within this wooden O the very casques / That did affright the air at Agincourt." Yet his theater rests on that figure, the wooden O within the universal O; and so did Renaissance statecraft.

As patrons of painting and drama, princes were not behindhand in adopting these scaenographic conventions for real palaces and cities. Their architects developed the city square as a theatrical orchestra, with a palace as the skene behind it and perspective avenues for entrances. In the passage quoted above from the *Four Books of Architecture*, Palladio advises his patrons to build their city center as a stage for the masques of secular power. His "military streets" are intended not only for the tactical conveyance of troops, but for their more effective display, and along such thoroughfares would be built the city's most imposing "fabrics" (palazzos and other large structures), to impress visitors with the city's wealth and power. These avenues converge on a theatrical piazza, with a palace for a backdrop. It is, he said, "a great ornament, when at the head of a street, a beautiful and spacious place is found, from which the prospect of some beautiful fabric is seen." Triumphal arches appear in Palladio's ideal city, but they are not to ride through, but to look through, along the axis of avenue and piazza. (Later, in the seventeenth century, the triumphal arch made its way into the theater as the proscenium arch, a looking-frame through which spectators might behold the heroic acts of kings.)

This histrionic vision of the state was leagued with an acceleration in building techniques to impose upon the city's complex web of physical and spiritual relationships the material imprint of geometric intellectual order.[15] In these plans one can see a mixture of religious and secular motives. Many of the famous street effects of Rome, for example, are the work of a series of planner popes in the fifteenth, sixteenth, and seventeenth centuries. Sixtus V designed a system of major avenues, connecting the city's most important shrines, to afford the pilgrim a straight way and a clear vision of his devotional goal. Nicholas V planned three parallel avenues as a formal approach to St. Peter's basilica, at once the goal of processions and a formidable symbol of the power of the quattrocento papacy. The most influential design was a famous "trident" at the Piazza del Populo, three avenues radiating at equal angles from a square inside the city gate. In the piazza, on the wedge-shaped spaces between the streets, twin churches were erected, their identical facades creating a symmetrical effect comparable to that in Palladio's Teatro Olimpico. (In the early twentieth century this composition was completed by the erection, at the end of the vista down the central avenue, of the most imposing fabric of them all, that shrine to the modern Italian state, the Tomb of Victor Emmanuel II.)

It may be that it is impossible to use such geometrical and radiocentric devices in city planning without summoning up the religious image of the city's center as the center of the earth, the place where the king is elevated into a god, and without inviting the people to come there and worship—to reverence either the prince or the idea of the holy state which he symbolizes. Jacques Perret's book of fortified axial cities was dedicated to Henri IV as "God's lieutenant on earth and the principal minister of His Glory." When political leadership removes itself into the realm of the aesthetic and presents itself as a dramatization of the religious search for perfection, it is no longer a practical art in touch with the reality of those whom it governs, nor is it in a position to recognize its own imperfection. Seeking unqualified admiration, it expects unqualified allegiance and promises unqualified felicity. Its success, rendered dramatically absolute, becomes the image of the millennium; its failure, a tragedy.

In the Renaissance, then, the visual symbols of power began to gravitate from the city's periphery to its center. Walls and gates started a long decline as measures of the king's might, gradually to be replaced by straight thoroughfares and centrally located squares with monumental facades for backdrops: volumes of open space controlled from one or a few points of vantage and offering the new delights of a long symmetrical perspective. Or the king's overseeing and harmonizing control might be realized in polygons and other regular and radiocentric arrangements so extensive that they could be apprehended only by an eye in the sky, that is, a map. To conceive the grandeur of one's city in its plan, rather than in the elevation of single gates, walls, or buildings, transforms completely Aristotle's criterion that a city should be *eusynoptos*, easily taken in by the eye. It asserts that there is only one proper point of view, a viewpoint that is outside of time. The ichnographic plan implies a simultaneous apprehension of all the quarters of the city. The straight perspective street offers always the same terminus to the eye, the obelisk or facade that screens the vanishing point. This new concept of urban space suppresses the fourth dimension, in which the street's aspect and prospect change dramatically as one moves along it, in which a variety of architectures proclaims the long duration of human indwelling.

The new treatment of space also represents a quantum leap in the potential accumulation and manipulation of secular power. Though some of Shakespeare's plays look back to the old image of the king as the citybreaker at the gates, others present in classic or medieval garb a representative scene of the Renaissance new order: a group of strongmen sectioning up a map. This scene is repeated in *Julius Caesar, 1 Henry IV,* and *King Lear.* Cleopatra's eulogium for Antony conveys the colossal and godlike pose of a man above a map, his eyes observing "the little O, the earth," his hands dispensing kingdoms like coins. The king with his architect consulting an ichnographic plan, the prince enjoying the perspective from his balcony, is the man visibly and visually *in charge.* The concert of polygons on the map, the theatrical vistas provided by the balcony's eminence, offer the same consolations of harmony with the absolute that auguries once offered to Romulus and Constantine. And the visual return invites the populace to acclaim him, lofty above them at the center of the world, as the dramatized epitome of that absolute. It is the triumph of aesthetics; the king has become a tragedian, the city a painting.

Except for the fortress towns, geometric construction in the Renaissance was confined to piecemeal efforts in existing cities. The Baroque age aspired to greater things—effects so immense as to be almost incomprehensible to the merely human viewer walking upon the earth. Then the plan or architectural model became not only an artwork but a cult object, like the shrine in the ancient city, a microcosm manifesting the city's ideal form, but not now for the imagination of every citizen; rather, it provided a few men at the center with a sense of spectatorial control. It unlocked to the king's eye the secret harmony of the vast compositions he had willed into being.

In a famous passage in the *Discourse on Method*, Descartes used the sense of overview in Baroque design as a metaphor for his own systematizing of thought:

We see that the buildings designed and completed by a single architect are usually more beautiful and better planned than those which many have tried to redesign, making do with old walls which had been built for other purposes. Thus those ancient towns which were nothing but hamlets in the beginning, and in the course of time have become great cities, are ordinarily . . . badly planned, compared to those regular districts that an engineer lays out on a plain according to his own imagination.[16]

Such unity of effect was the aim of the Baroque. Improving technology could make building a city like painting a picture, something one strong-willed man could accomplish in a short span of years and then step back from and admire. Or, if necessary, an immense but clearly conceived plan could be executed over several lifetimes and yet preserve the signature of its originator's imagination. As a symbol of immortality and perfection, the ideal city was not to suggest the mutations and reversals of history. Any change of architectural orders, any made-over or misaligned building, would reveal that the city is not a simple and divinely ordained space, but a dynamic superimposition and coordination of diverse existential spaces occupied by diversely motivated humans over many years. To perceive the latter city, however, one must dwell there, on the ground, rather than standing somewhere overhead.[17] From the mapmaker's lofty vantage point, those many layers of human memory, sentiment, social cohesion, and quotidian intercourse are almost imperceptible. A little demolition will erase them. It is best, therefore, that the physical terrain of the city be leveled too, in imitation of a canvas or map; for a ridge or hill, like a wrinkle on paper, can deflect the pen or the eye and suggest that inhabited space is different from the homogeneous conceptual medium of a Newton and a Descartes.

Descartes, of course, continued, "We do not see men destroying all the houses of a city for the sole purpose of remaking them in another way, and rendering the streets more beautiful." But the princely cartesians of his own age, and of more recent times, often did just that, tracing their lines of force directly through the city's homes.

In seventeenth-century England, however, those layers of inhabitation proved too much for the abstract designs of Descartes's fellow mathematician Christopher Wren. When the Great Fire erased most of the ancient, labyrinthine City of London, Wren executed a new plan overnight, simply by drawing avenues from the old city gates and London Bridge to converge on the Royal Exchange. Within twelve days from the subsiding of the fire, he and at least three competitors traced various grids and stars upon what seemed to them the blank map of inner London, and addressed their works to King Charles.

Their plans proved to be only *città ideali*, however, artistic compliments paid to the king. What defeated them was their indifference not to physical topography, but to the spiritual landscape of old London. In Charles's quick interest in these schemes and his equally quick retreat to an arrangement for regulated reconstruction on the old plan, we see the conflict between two versions of sacral places, one depending on the power of a visually seductive plan and an autocratic prince, the other resting on inhabitation, ritual, and years of psychological indwelling. The new city rose in a style almost as irregular as the old; London thus has remained one of the very few capital cities lacking an apparatus of processional avenues leading to a dramatic "center."

The great mapmaker triumphs of the seventeenth century were mainly built where topographical and bourgeois resistance were at a minimum. With an important exception to be discussed later, Louis XIV ignored Paris as a tablet for the imprint of his power and occupied himself with the fortress cities on the frontiers of France and with his garden-city at Versailles. Sebastien le Prestre de Vauban, his designer of citadels, and André Le Nôtre, his garden architect, understood perfectly the psychology of absolutism, with its attraction to the geometric plan and the dramatic perspective.

Vauban threw around France a ring of cities encrusted in the elaborate geometric system of rampart, ditch, and glacis—a system he had perfected to counter the sophisticated techniques for siege which he had himself developed. He urged Louis to think *"en grand,"* to conceive his kingdom as an abstract homogeneous space with sharply defined boundaries. That was how Vauban viewed cities. Though he did fortify some preexisting cities, notably Strasbourg, Vauban's preference was for the garrison city, executed on a clean level site and ringed with a mile or so of cleared space. His masterpiece, Neuf-Brisach, is a regular octagon with an immense square *place d'armes* at the center—"the forum for a city of soldiers" is one architectural historian's apt comment.[18] From that square, four straight avenues extend to the gates, efficiently routing men and munitions to the point of attack.

Fortification, Vauban said, had higher designs than mere efficiency: "the beautiful symmetry and solidity of its ramparts" should assert to foreigners the magnificence of the king of France.[19] Defenses had by this time grown so complex, the ring of works so thick, that their "symmetry" was apparent not so much on the site (that is, in elevation) as in an inspection of the plan—which means that it was visible to military engineers, to statesmen, and to the king. As Perret and Palladio had dedicated books to their patron kings, Vauban dedicated completed fortresses, with a lapidary inscription at the gates identifying Louis as founder and benefactor. Vauban's city is a military stronghold, but it is also a vehicle of psychological power based on the king's sense that such cities are artifacts, intricate objects of virtu created at his will to serve a single, centralized design which he alone can discern. Turbulent, unfocused Paris in his time was not such a city, so Louis demolished its ramparts and moved to Versailles, there to create an appropriate stage for his role as *le Roi Soleil*, sovereign of France.

At Versailles the cult of the plan and the cult of the perspective combined with Louis's statecraft to make his residence the city at the center of the world. On the west side of the palace was marshaled a world of nature: a parterre of clipped grass, symmetrical walkways, carefully regimented trees and water. On the east stood an equally regulated human society: a large parade ground and beyond that a small city for the king's ministerial officials. The city was divided into four sectors by three avenues radiating from the *place d'armes*. The buildings along the avenues, uniform in height and style, enhanced the sense of perspective, and the residents were assigned to sectors according to social rank and ministerial affiliation.[20] West, beyond the parterre and the canals, extended a large hunting park, sectored like the city by three converging alleys. These alleys and the city's avenues thus create a radiocentric pattern converging on the palace. Louis had created for himself a harmonious world at Versailles, a world where he was clearly and dramatically at the center, a world to which all had to come who wished to benefit by the divine power which he transmitted to men. The poet La Fontaine averred that Louis had created a world for himself;[21] in his *Memoirs* the king modestly denied this, saying that rather he wished "to understand everything." Kingship, he advised his son, "consists of keeping an eye on the whole world, . . . of seeing around us what has been hidden from us with the greatest care."[22]

Like the plan of Neuf-Brisach, much of the effect of Versailles escapes direct visual experience. It is too large. Also, the seemingly thick forestation outlining the upper parterres and the Allée Royale conceals within it a system of geometric pathways converging on *bosquets*, small bowers cleared within the wood and filled with fountains and statuary, in a variety of motifs—stars, labyrinths, quincunxes, amphitheaters, "ballrooms." Modern aerial photography, done in wintertime, can reveal something of the complexity of Le Nôtre's total design, but in 1680 it could have been comprehended only in the planner's mind—and in Louis's, for whom this great *bibelot* was built:

> A plank was placed across two horses to provide a table, and there Le Nôtre spread out the first of his plans. The King looked at it, was pleased, and said, "Le Nôtre, for this I will give you twenty thousand *livres*."[23]

The plan's the thing; with it, Louis takes possession before ever a stone is set or a tree planted. And when the work is done, he remains —thanks to his plan—still literally the overseer. Appropriate to Versailles was Louis's royal device, that eye in the sky, the sun.

Le Roi Soleil: not only a point of view, but a role to play. Little need be said about the theatrical sense of this monarch, so often a ruinous influence on his conduct of foreign affairs and fiscal policy. Versailles was dedicated in 1664 with a week-long masque, *The Pleasures of the Enchanted Isle*, written by Moliére, in which Louis acted the role of the hero. The palace was to be indeed his enchanted isle, removed from Paris's political hazards. Moreover, as a great stage, Versailles detached the king's acts from ordinary life. It set him at an aesthetic distance from his subjects. The court's poetry, the garden sculpture, the design of the grounds, all contributed to an allegory of the King as Apollo, the sun god. La Fontaine wrote:

When the Sun is tired, his work done,
He descends to Tethys and takes his rest.
So also Louis comes, putting aside
The care that every day he must resume.
. . . .
Here, in golden carriages the Prince and court
Come to taste the freshness of the evening.
The one Sun and the Other, each unique in his sphere,
Manifest to all their wealth and grandeur.[24]

In that theatrical setting, as in Palladio's, perspective was an important consideration. Louis was intensely conscious of it. He set down in his own handwriting a guide, *How To Show the Gardens at Versailles*, providing an itinerary with pauses at the most striking vantage points, all of which offer bilaterally symmetrical perspectives.[25] Along each vista, jets of water and statues are used like gunsights to enforce the symmetry and to assure the viewer that he is in a most favored position, where everything falls into line: that he stands at the center of the world. Analyzing the work of Le Nôtre, the garden historian Derek Clifford describes his vista garden as "an enormous carpet laid from the home terrace into a distance so remote that it seemed a backcloth rather than a reality. [It] had the particular unreality of the theatre: its major coherent purpose was to stun not to charm."[26]

Richard Wilbur, whose poetry often turns on the psychology of architecture, reads a countermessage in Versailles:

They built well who made
Those palaces of hunting lords, the grounds planned
  As ruled reaches, always with a view
  Down tapered aisles of trees at last to fade
    In the world's mass. The lords so knew
      Of land beyond their land.

      If, at Versailles, outdrawn
By the stairs or the still canals, by the gradual shrink of an urn
  Or the thousand fountains, a king gave back his gaze
  To the ample balanced windows vantaged on
    The clearness near, and the far haze,
      He learned he must return.[27]

Aware of the dangers of transforming life into art, Wilbur reads in Baroque perspectives an antitheater diminishing the king's sense of absolute power: the visual return to the palace—which Louis notes in his guide—in Wilbur's poem admonishes him to return from his irresponsible garden-drama of absolute power, to take up the imperfect governance of a finite kingdom. Like Wilbur, Lewis Mumford sees the long perspective avenue as belittling the king by removing him and his palace to the vanishing point.[28] The histrionic use of perspective obviously has limits; Bernini—who had done work for the stage—understood this, for in designing the piazza before St. Peter's he called for its complete enclosure by a colonnade to limit the distance from which the basilica could be viewed, and thus to guarantee its overtowering impressiveness.[29] At Versailles the east-west axis of the Allée Royale and the Avenue de Paris was eventually extended more than eleven kilometers. With the eclipse of the encircling wall as a symbol of power, the radial design surrendered completely to Baroque expansiveness. Yet Louis, at the center of his composition and in imaginative control of it, seems to have found the design aggrandizing rather than belittling; so must his contemporaries, for Versailles, its gardens and its radial urban plan, dominated the design of residence cities for a century: St. Petersburg (Leningrad), Karlsruhe, and Washington are three of the best known.

The cities of Louis and of Peter the Great represent an apogee in the building of cities for the king's custom. By comparison, such later—and larger—achievements as the geometrizing of Paris and Washington seem depersonalized, the working out or the extension of designs made not by the imperious edict of one overseeing king, but by bureaucrats and committees motivated by some sense of national history and identity which they sought to incarnate in the capital city.

The development of modern Paris reflects the homogeneous architectural vision of three quite different monarchies. Le Nôtre's first commission from Louis XIV was to redesign the gardens between the Tuileries Palace and the city wall. He leveled the site, drew a central avenue perpendicular to the palace facade, and planted the garden symmetrically along that axis. Then, in an easy landscaper's gesture, he extended its vista beyond the city wall, planting a double row of trees across the open fields to a hilltop, where he set up an obelisk.[30] Sixty years later a road was opened between the trees, called the Champs-Élysées. Another thirty years, and a square (now the Place de la Concorde) was built to join that parkway with the Tuileries. At its center, on line with the garden's avenue and the obelisk, stood an equestrian statue of Louis XV. The hilltop was later flattened and called the Place de l'Étoile. Thus an organizing vista in a royal garden had become the baseline, three kilometers long, for Euclidizing the whole northwest quarter of Paris two hundred years later.

Napoleon's urge to sacralize his power assumed the same Graeco-Roman decor as the Bourbons'. He commenced an Arch of Triumph on the Étoile and another behind the Tuileries, both straddling Le Nôtre's line. He bisected that line with a shorter vista running from the Madeleine—a classical Temple of Glory for his armies—through the square that had been Louis XV's, across the Seine to a facade of Corinthian columns grafted on the rear of the old Bourbon Palace, which happened to stand conveniently, but out of alignment, at the other end of the bridge. South of the river he set up the separate mechanisms of the Champs de Mars and the Avenue de l'Observatoire. He could give Paris no single visual center, but he clarified several interlocked perspectives terminating in shrines to the military or to the empire. His citybuilding, like his empire, had little to do with the mundane needs of Paris.

Napoleon III and his prefect, Baron Haussmann, on the other hand, combined a real sense of human needs with their interest in military convenience and imperial honorifics. Everyone has heard that their avenues and boulevards, converging on round points, were true Palladian "military streets" intended for crowd control because they were straight enough for cannon fire, too wide to barricade, and paved in asphalt, which could not be torn up and thrown at troops; and because they encircled or broke apart neighborhoods notorious for insurrection. But Napoleon and Haussmann also conceived of them as a great public works program, not only providing employment but also improving living conditions by demolishing slums, by introducing light and air into the inner-city labyrinth, and by making traffic faster and safer. They were of a piece with less conspicuous achievements like the public parks, the new sewage system, and the safe water supply.[31]

At the same time, though, the rebuilding of Paris had other

motives than the utilitarian. It embodied again the desire of post-medieval kings to dramatize their power by displaying visual control over the city—either at the center of perspective avenues, or in the abstract space of the plan. The new Paris began with maps. When Haussmann took office as Prefect of the Seine, Louis Napoleon gave him a map of the city on which he had crayoned the new streets he planned to build, with a color scheme corresponding to their urgency. The prefect next made an up-to-date planimetric and topographical survey of Paris, which he then mounted on an immense frame in his office. He spent, he said, many hours "in fruitful meditation before this altar-screen."[32] His next task was to make the actual terrain of the city resemble the map as much as possible by flattening out its irregularities, whether for practical effects (to facilitate a new street intersection) or for aesthetics (to lengthen a vista).

In building the new boulevards and avenues, the prefect frequently manipulated construction so as to achieve a striking visual effect at the end of the street. He aimed the Boulevard St.-Michel at the ancient spire of Sainte-Chapelle, and sited the new Tribunal de Commerce so that its dome—placed at one side of the building! —would terminate the Boulevard de Sébastopol.[33] On the Île de la Cité, which he cleared and rebuilt as a precinct for municipal administration, he opened in front of Notre Dame an area as large as the cathedral itself, to give it a proper viewing-space. As the religious center of the medieval city that had once huddled around the Île, the cathedral had embodied for the faithful the kinetic experience of a translation from one world to another, from chaos to order, from common light into illumination, from the profane into the sacred. Now, as a facade at the end of a square, it became another of Haussmann's visual effects, one of the several depots of civil comfort grouped on his island in the Seine.

On the right bank of the river Louis Napoleon extended the Louvre till it met the Tuileries Palace, thus completing an imperial enclave begun more than six hundred years before, enclosing a great rectangle and creating the appearance of its axial arrangement along Le Nôtre's old linear drawn from the gardens to the Étoile.[34] This precinct, and its environs, served as the stage of the Liberal Empire. Like his predecessors, Louis had a taste for theatrics. Fancy dress balls dominated the winter season at the Tuileries, their costumes often derived from the opera or the opera-bouffe of the day. Amateur theatricals and charades filled in between balls. The Universal Exposition of 1867, staged on the Champs de Mars nearby, was itself an episode in kitsch theater, distracting the country from its deteriorating international position. To the north was the new opera house, also opened in 1867, surrounded by streets named for popular composers and librettists and approached by an avenue—another of Haussmann's compositions—named for the role which Louis Bonaparte had chosen for himself to play in the grand opera of his empire: the Avenue Napoleon.[35]

The rebuilt Place de l'Étoile was one of Haussmann's showplaces. This great asterisk at the end of the Champs-Élysées was built for imperial display rather than for the efficient circulation of traffic. There the prefect asserted all his power to regularize the city's design. To an irregular quadratic intersection he added no fewer than eight new avenues, so sited as to create a perfectly regular twelve-pointed star. Like Versailles, the conception is so grand as to be comprehensible only from above—from atop the arch, or better, from a map, colored perhaps to reveal the progress of one's grand design. Crowned with Napoleon's arch, consecrated with the remains of France's unknown soldier, and now named for Charles de Gaulle, the point where Le Nôtre's eye met the horizon has become a shrine to national military glory.

The Paris achieved by this succession of princes and their managers influenced one minor episode of the career of another connoisseur of the melodramatic, Adolf Hitler. In the summer of 1936, Albert Speer writes in his memoirs, Hitler gave him plans and drawings for a triumphal avenue through the heart of Berlin. It was to be enormously wide, 140 meters, and nearly 5 kilometers in length. Its southern terminus was an immense arch of triumph before a railway station, the northern a domed meeting hall "into which St. Peter's Cathedral in Rome would have fitted several times over," approached across a traffic-free square (Adolf-Hitler Platz) which would hold a million people. Flanking the square were the Chancellery and the High Command. Here in megascopic purity are the ceremonial gate, the military street (to be lined with captured tanks and cannon), the cleared and regularly bounded space, and finally the pantheon with its theatrical facade and, inside, its inevitable balcony. Hitler, Speer writes, had been impressed by the achievements of Haussmann. "The Champs-Élysées with its Arc de Triomphe . . . was the model for his great arch and for the width of his avenue as well." Speer describes Hitler's gift for drafting and illustrating his architectural ideas, and says "At bottom, I think, his sense of political mission and his passion for architecture were always inseparable."[36]

Part of this design, as humanized by Speer and the Traffic Minister Liebbrand, was actually built. But most of Hitler's Berlin was realized only in some extensive models, which he kept in guarded rooms of the Chancellery. Speer has left us a valuable portrait of Hitler as colossus:

> Hitler was particularly excited over a large model of the grand boulevard on a scale of 1:1000. He loved to "enter his avenue" at various points and take measure of the future effect. . . . To do so, he bent down, almost kneeling, his eye an inch or so above the level of the model, in order to have the right perspective, and while looking he spoke with unusual vivacity.[37]

Hitler's immense toy, probably the most harmless of his designs, no doubt returned him more pleasure than would the completed fabric. Speer describes his own design for the vast assembly hall, and for the Führer's podium, situated beneath an immense German eagle; but he confesses to an old problem, the reduction of the hero by perspective:

> I tried to give this spot suitable emphasis, but here the fatal flaw of architecture that has lost all sense of proportion was revealed. Under that vast dome Hitler dwindled to an optical zero.[38]

Speer, correctly analyzing the hall as "a place of worship . . . essentially pseudoreligious," suggests that the object of worship was rather more than the person of the Führer himself. Hitler, he says, thought of his structures as serving the German nation in the future as the classical and Renaissance architecture of Rome was then serving the Italians. Acquiring psychological power over the course of centuries, these works would manifest national identity to the later Reich, just as historic Rome symbolized the glories of Italy, through the person of Mussolini, for those who gathered in the Piazza Venezia, below the Tomb of Victor Emmanuel on the

Capitoline Hill. The sacral motive was thus depersonalized, the invitation to worship shifted back from prince to idea, in this case an abstract *Volksgeist*, which the folk might worship in their own unity beneath that great pantheon dome.[39] And this depersonalization confers immortality as well: deeds done for the Reich are done in fabrication of a sacred history, ordained by fate but yet to be written, extending over a thousand years the order conceived in microcosm here, in space, in the stupendous volumes of avenue, square, and assembly hall.

In Peking, the Maoist government has accomplished exactly what Hitler had planned. During all the old regimes the Gate of Heavenly Peace had stood between the teeming confusion of the Inner City and the cosmic order of the Imperial City, that nest of shrines discussed in chapter 1. Like the portals of a medieval cathedral, the gate symbolized a translation from the profane to the sacred. Now an immense People's Square has been opened in front of it, approached not only by the old processional way from the south but also by a wide parade route running east and west. In its center, along an extension of that geomancer's line which served as axis of the Imperial City, stand the mausoleum of Mao Tse-tung and a stele inscribed, "The People's Heroes Are Immortal." The square is flanked by a museum of Chinese history and by a large assembly hall, each 400 meters in length. And so the gate has become the backdrop of a stupendous religio-political theater. Its upper story serves, like the balcony in the occidental theater or piazza, as a reviewing stand and display case for the leaders of the People's Republic. But they are appropriately overwhelmed by the mass rallies in the square, where the people celebrate the magnitude of their power and the long reach of their history and their history to be. And the Imperial City's arcana have been opened for all to inspect. The drama of the people's assembly now makes visually manifest that which the city's cosmological plan had once realized through symbol, in the imagination: the old ethnocentric ideal of a Middle Kingdom surrounded by hostile forces.

America's *città ideale*, Washington, reveals how plan and perspective can triumph even in the seeming eclipse of princes. Conceived in a mixture of democratic and autocratic motives at the end of the eighteenth century, it was revised during the nation's coming of age one hundred years later and continues to evolve today, ever more singlemindedly dominating the Potomac landscape. In its history one looks in vain for a prince or a succession of strongmen; the development of Washington as the symbol of a democracy's power has rested in the hands of committees, appointees, commissioners, and other civil servants. Yet it has developed inexorably into a theater and a shrine for abstract national goals.

In 1791 George Washington established the Federal District on farmland along the Potomac River. What kind of capital city should a democratic republic have? Ignoring an unpretentious gridiron plan submitted by Thomas Jefferson, the president appointed a special designer, Pierre Charles L'Enfant, who had come to America in 1777 as a military engineer, and who proposed to plan for the long-range growth of a city sure to become "the Capital of a powerful Empire."[40] After a summer's work on the Potomac site, L'Enfant set before the president a design which combined a gridiron with a system of radiocentric avenues deriving from two principal foci, the "President's Palace" and the "Congress House," and from several subordinate squares and bridgeheads.

This design is in the tradition of the *città ideale.* The son of a court painter at Versailles, L'Enfant had spent his youth in Paris and was familiar both with the architecture of pomp and with the expected style of an artist toward his patron. His plan advises Washington, as Vauban had Louis XIV, to think *en grand.* It encompasses the whole Federal District in a master plan more suited to future expansion than to the tiny settlement which federal government would require in 1800. The map is color coded in blue, green, yellow, and two shades of red, and its margins carry explanations and lists of buildings, monuments, and parks keyed to the map. Like a painting, it puts the patron in imaginative possession of the city's full natural site, while the marginalia describe details and propose a system for colonization. These notes specify the subject of just one monument: an "equestrian figure of GEORGE WASHINGTON." Two "historic columns," a national church, and fifteen squares are reserved for memorials of future events and of heroes yet unborn. Through them Washington is placed at the fountainhead of a future already treated as history. Though drafted before the city's name was formally proposed, the map thus dedicates to George Washington the national capital, placing it at his command in both space and time.

L'Enfant arranged his streets and buildings to symbolize federal power and to provide for its theatrical display. The generative center of his composition is a right triangle. At one of its acute angles, on a slope above the Potomac, stands the President's Palace. At the other acute angle, to the southeast, the Congress House occupies a commanding hill. The two structures would "serve as models for all subsequent undertakings, and stand to future ages a monument to national genius." A "magnificent grand avenue" more than two kilometers long would connect them, by sight as well as by carriage. A long garden south from the palace would meet another avenue extending west from Congress's hill. At the point of intersection, the triangle's right angle, would stand that "grand equestrian figure" of Washington, near the shore of a Potomac far wider then than it is today. The triangle thus enshrines Congress in its deliberative and corporate presence and the Executive in his personal, residential character, and unites both with the city's eponym, Washington. The arrangement of diagonal streets had also a symbolic value. Each front of the two federal structures commands a trident of vistas, like that at Versailles, piercing through the city toward its limits. This city, like the constitution that authorized it, draws attention and power to the federal center.[41]

That the third point of the central triangle should be Washington's memorial statue, not the Supreme Court, is consonant with the importance which the plan's notes attach to monuments not only to commemorate a history yet unmade, but also to define and disseminate a national character by perpetuating the memory of "those whose usefulness hath rendered them worthy of general imitation, to invite the youth of succeeding generations to tread in the paths of those sages or heroes."[42] L'Enfant's plan, which established a thousand blocks for an imperial metropolis, also provided the empty tablets for a national history conceived as patriotic allegory both moral and anagogical. His city would immortalize an idea, *Americanitas.*

There was, however, a counterforce in L'Enfant's design. The engineer's letters reveal his sensitivity to the picturesque setting of the proposed capital, encircled by hills and looking out on a long reach of the Potomac. Unlike the similar compositions at Versailles and Paris, the perspectives in L'Enfant's city were not all to be closed theatrically by an imperious facade. Some were to remain open to the river or the countryside; the architectural details in the foreground serving, as in a Poussin painting, to provide contrasting verticals and angular contours. Le Nôtre's compulsion to expand formal symmetries to the horizon is absent. West and south the city's avenues would reveal an untidy and dynamic landscape of hills, river, and the port at Alexandria. These centrifugal perspectives set a limit to the city's architectural assertion of order and control. In Wilbur's phrase, they tell of land beyond the rulers' land.[43]

Limitations on federal power seemed unnecessary and were forgotten early in the nineteenth century. L'Enfant's map disappeared, and all his planned visual effects were canceled by uncoordinated building. On each of the legs of the central triangle there appeared large structures to intercept the view: the Treasury on Pennsylvania Avenue; the colossal obelisk raised in the Mall instead of a small equestrian statue of Washington; even a railway station that transversed the Mall at the foot of Capitol Hill. In the last decades of the century the silted-up tidal flats of the Potomac west and south of the Washington Monument were reclaimed for a park, so that the obelisk stood at the center of a tract of public land, rather than at the corner.

Then the frontier closed; the United States inherited Spain's colonial territories; and, as Henry Adams said, "the climax of empire could be seen approaching"[44]—the empire for which L'Enfant had designed his city. As Washington's centennial approached, James McMillan, chairman of the Senate Committee on the District of Columbia, set up a commission to study ways to incorporate the new parkland beyond the monument and to beautify the city in a style consistent with the original plan, recently rediscovered. L'Enfant's architectural executor was to be not an individual but, suitably for a democracy, a committee. To his commission McMillan appointed the men who had designed the fairgrounds for the Chicago Columbian Exposition of 1893. That white city, conceived in neoclassical idiom and executed largely in glittering white plaster over lath, spoke to turn-of-the-century America as the image of its millennial future. On the now-muddled map of central Washington, these men traced the old quadratic of sacralized civil power:

a symmetrical, polygonal, or kite-shaped, figure bisected from east to west by the axis of the Capitol and from north to south by the White House axis. Regarding the Monument as the center, the Capitol as the base, and the White House as the extremity of one arm of a Latin cross, we have at the head of the composition on the banks of the Potomac a memorial site of the grandest possible dignity, with a second and only less commanding site at the extremity of the second arm.[45]

In an aerial perspective illustrating their proposal, this enclave appears as holy ground, swept clean of profane structures, and bathed in a brilliant light. Its buildings are all neoclassical, all gleaming white. Beyond, cast in impenetrable shadow, lies the Washington of residence and commerce, of embassy, lobby and salon—that Washington which Henry James called "the City of Conversation." The vistas of their quincunx open only toward the other monuments, admitting nothing that lies beyond—not the river, not the Virginia shore, not the City of Conversation. This design emphasizes whatever in L'Enfant's plan was centripetal and self-contained, everything that would make the capital a memorial to the nation's symbolic history and an expositor of the principles of its government: the Rome of a democratic *imperium.*

The architects Daniel Burnham and Charles McKim designated the western arm as the site of a memorial for Abraham Lincoln. Their vaguely defined grouping of buildings at the southern point was never developed, and in the 1930s a memorial for Jefferson rose there instead. These two cenotaphs have assumed the exemplary tone L'Enfant desired, immortalizing not the men themselves, nor even their ideas—though they present statues, and ideas graven on the walls—but rather subsuming men and ideas to a depersonalized and almost ineffable vision of national principle. Thus two points of the new quadratic symbolize the mythohistorical expression of America's ideals, as the other two symbolize the major agencies of a republican democracy.

At the center rises the obelisk, a symbol so pure that it need not represent even the appearance or the words of the founder president. Though the monument had been completed some fifteen years earlier, the McMillan plan established a setting in which it found an appropriateness it had not enjoyed in the earlier triangular arrangement. For the city had been originally laid out on a grand scale commensurate with the dim picturesque distances L'Enfant sought to frame; when buildings were introduced at the new extremities of the composition, they were so distant from one another that their formal relationship would not have been perceptible to a person on the ground. To achieve the visual control which this design requires for appreciation, one must see it from above.

Although it was necessary for the commission and its legatees to court by any and all means the attention and favor of presidents and congressmen, providing them with the customary models and aerial-view sketches, it is finally not for the flattery of presidents and congressmen that the grandeur of Washington is intended. Hence the importance of the Washington Monument in Burnham and McKim's plan. The obelisks in the Place de la Concorde and the Piazza del Populo are relatively small and solid sighting points for pedestrian observers. This monument is tall and hollow, having an interior stair and elevator mounting to an observation deck. The commanding eye for whom the design is made is not the president's in his oval office, nor the senator's on the terraces of the Capitol, nor indeed the eye in glory that tops the pyramid on the Great Seal, but the eye of the American pilgrim, the ordinary citizen, come to Washington to find his place in the national allegory. From windows at the pinnacle of this *axis mundi,* he may behold the four-square cosmos that lies quartered beneath his feet and so may perhaps attain to a vision of the power of the secular state to compel all things into unity. As interpreted by the commission, the message of Washington was frankly symbolic and conceptual. Once the lines of sight are made clear, one "understands" it as a statement about the ideologies of American history and American government.

That it aggrandized an idea rather than a person is characteristically American, and so has been the execution of the plan, carried out by a succession of presidents, committees, and commissions, none seeking personal immortality, for all the residents of inner Washington are transients. The efforts of the last seventy-five years, often put back by war or depression, have gone to secure and to expand the perimeter of the federal enclave, to expel from it all structures serving a profane (i.e., neither constitutional nor commemorative nor repository) function, and to enforce a homogeneous neoclassical architecture on new construction. Until this style was modified on two or three recent museums, it was difficult to tell by appearance the relative age of the structures, though the Jefferson Memorial is nearly 140 years younger than the White House opposite it. Perhaps the Mall today most resembles a Hollywood designer's rendering of the Roman forum. Such homogeneity or "flatness" of facade, an achievement chronologically paralleling the development of convenient popular photography, has produced in Washington a diorama city in which the foreground figure is neither Renaissance prince nor nineteenth-century emperor, but the American citizen, who may not really see the Capitol until, at home again, he beholds it towering behind the tiny cluster of his family as he reviews his slides.

The same interest in arranging a backdrop has affected the renovation of Pennsylvania Avenue, L'Enfant's grand carriageway. A presidential Act in 1965 affirmed that "the segment of Pennsylvania Avenue between the White House and the Capitol has symbolized the majesty and power of the American Republic and the triumphs and tragedies of the American people."[46] In 1900 it was lined with structures in various vernacular architectures, in all stages of elegance and dilapidation, serving the assorted profane purposes of the citizens of the capital. The McMillan Commission found this ragtag company "entirely unworthy of the conspicuous positions they occupy"; and, on the south side of the avenue, where they recommended the construction of municipal buildings, now stand the huge uniform blocks of the Federal Triangle, housing many of the bureaucracies associated with the executive branch. In the 1960s another commission drew up a plan to extend federal buildings along the north side also, so as to create continuous and architecturally harmonious facades the entire length of the avenue, like those in a theater set of Serlio's. The commission explained the motive:

> To the millions who know Washington on television, the visual quality of the city will be enormously enhanced. . . . Ornamental paving, special street furniture and lighting, street graphics, fountains and sculpture, arcaded buildings of uniform setback and height but for varying purposes announced in their architectures—these will create a richly designed special street whose excitement will be communicated as a strong image even to those who may never see it in reality.[47]

Thus, while the plan does propose set-in balconies for some of the new buildings, the true balcony and reviewing stand of the avenue will be the television set in every American home, actualizing there the majesty and power of the Republic. Perhaps television can even solve the problem—noted by Mumford, Wilbur, and Speer—of how perspective diminishes the hero on his colossal stage. With its capacity to absorb an event through a dozen cameras, television can command simultaneously events on several stages—Capitol, Avenue, White House—and in a variety of depths from panorama to closeup. While the Renaissance single-perspective scene is thus broken up technically, it is reunified in the sensorium of the viewer, who, through his unseen managers the scenarist and the director, commands the scene more fully than the mere president, and replaces him as the colossal hero on the 19-inch stage. While a mass society like America's dissolves those intermediate social groups which might extrinsically confirm a citizen's worth, the electronic mass media make him prince, by aestheticizing his own sensations. Of this new prince, more will be said in the next chapter.

"Make no little plans," wrote Daniel Burnham, "make big plans . . . remembering that a noble, logical diagram once recorded will never die, but long after we are gone will be a living thing, asserting itself with ever-growing insistency."[48] From rites of consecration and from military convenience arose in antiquity an ideal, orthogonal city plan laying stress on a continuous boundary containing a four-quartered, four-gated model of the cosmos, its center the vertical *axis mundi* where mortals might attain the transcendent. In antiquity such an ideal was seldom realized, except for a time in some new town built from a Roman army camp; in the Middle Ages that cosmological intent gave shape to the interiors of churches rather than to actual cities. To those times, a building's height or a city's gates expressed more fully the magnificence of its polity.

The Renaissance, however, began to conceive space more abstractly. From paper plans for the *città ideale,* from the discovery of the techniques for rendering perspective, and from a developing political and technical skill that offered results quick enough for mortal princes to enjoy, there developed a style of building new cities, or rebuilding old, in a geometric form which laid the city before one man's commanding eye—an eye more and more remote from the dynamic uncertainties and discoveries of the walker in the medieval town, more and more detached into an eye in the sky, viewing a map or a clutch of radial avenues beneath his balcony. The new design offered a visual clarity which the older cities, more kinetically conceived, did not. Planners, like ministers of state, encouraged their lords to think *en grand,* to straddle the whole space at once. The city's gates became subordinate to its streets and squares, newly conceived as a theater for the display of power; a city, like a post-Gutenberg poem, was becoming a manipulation of open space. In transforming the city into a simulacrum of a map, the designers sought to minimize not only the third dimension of its eccentric terrain, but also the fourth dimension as well, both by rendering it instantly accessible to the eye and by postulating a homogeneity of architectural style—usually the classical—in which the city becomes an artist's single act rather than a record of the successive and various acts of the generations who have dwelt there.

Thus—and again like the Renaissance poet—the city planner could flatter his patron with a promise of timelessness in his plan and with immortality through and beyond the plan as well. On the one hand, geometrical plans have proven irresistably "logical": they can extend and intensify themselves indefinitely, running an axial line to the horizon, filling in the city's center with symmetrical facades. Often conceiving the city as lines on paper, planners in the ideal tradition have seldom hesitated to erase old patterns of inhabitation, to sketch in new geometrics, and to dictate the social class and habits of their residents. On the other hand, the orthogonal diagram has, as Burnham said once, "magic to stir men's blood": appealing to an apparently primordial instinct for the sacred place, the radiocentric city invites men to come to its center and worship the power—now a secular one—that has impelled the city into being. As a decisive move in the long game between churchmen and princes, the state has commandeered the earthly image of the New Jerusalem for millennial purposes of its own. It has corrupted its own secularism with an iconography of religious devotion. In its insistence on visual effects and visual control, this architecture of power makes the city a spectacle for the king's inspection and the king a spectacle for the city's admiration. In the distanced, aesthetic realm created by a dominance of visual imagery, a merely fallible governance of merely imperfect men becomes unthinkable. Today the viewpoint of the Renaissance perspective has been reversed; the prince has vanished into the distance. Taking the view atop the Arc de Triomphe or the Washington Monument, thronged in a rally in Adolf-Hitler Platz or in the People's Square before the Gate of Heavenly Peace, or beholding his own sensations on the television, mass man may say, with all the self-worshipful complacency of a Bourbon, *l'état, c'est nous.*

The City of Man, said Augustine, seeks a peace after its own heart. It offers a self-contained eschatology, like a theater. It is not what Augustine thought a *civitas* ought to be, a community unified in pursuit of a goal beyond itself—"beyond," not in space at all, but in time. Human community has a dimension invisible on the city of paper: the dimension of discourse and its medium, time. Jesus turned back Satan with a word.

4: Where Will the Word Resound?

> *There are three parts to architecture: the design of buildings, the making of timepieces, and the construction of machinery.*
>
> Vitruvius, *The Ten Books of Architecture,* 1. 3. 1.

"SHRINE," "FORTRESS," "CYNOSURE," AND "THEATER": FOUR variations on the holy city, four visions of the spiritual life. As a primarily spatial image in words, in paint, or in stone and concrete, this city stands outside of time, its streets often empty or, sometimes, thronged with a strangely unanimous citizenry. It is a macrocosmic emblem of the soul, or of some indivisible spiritual principle. If extended, "allegorically," to represent corporate holiness—a church or a divinely chosen nation—the image denies the imaginative reality of the secular place and time in which the religious community is set.

Of course, the holy city may be cast into time by an extension of space. Withdrawn into an eschatological distance, it sets the worshiper on the road, as pilgrim and alien, and turns the secular world into the Time Being. The pilgrim's imagination keeps Jerusalem in view while the feet follow, stumbling, the byways of time. But on the endless plains, ringed by the flat horizon, the city over the mountains may become unreal, shimmering and disintegrating like a mirage. An autocrat's literalism may reassemble that image in the Place d'Armes at Versailles, in the Adolf-Hitler Platz or People's Square, or in the televised image of Pennsylvania Avenue. Once more it becomes a symbol referring not to time, but to the immortality of a mythologized national history.

The city is where man lives in time: its life is the measure and record of time on a human scale. To render a religious experience

that is timebound and corporate—that is "urban"—we must add
to the city's visual image another dimension. We discover this dimension, which is the dimension of the soul, in the evanescence of
sound, in the summons of the human voice. The city in time, the
holy city *in saeculo,* is a place where the voice may resound; the
City of Man is a city in flight from time, whose noise conceals a terrible silence.

In the Zion psalms, and in the apocalyptic visions of the
prophets, the voice of God thunders over the citadel; it promises
victory, it renews the covenant, it shatters enemies without, it
judges the traitors within. It is the sound of power, the voice of the
king. Whether nationalistic or psychological in their symbolism,
these poems make the voice of God part of the city's wall, the
power that excludes evil and secures peace. But many of the psalms
of personal adversity—whether nationalistic or psychological—
begin instead from the intolerable silence of God: "Yahweh, hear
my voice as I cry! / Pity me! Answer me!" (Ps. 27:7). But the citadel echoes with other sounds, the noises of faction, the taunts of
conspirators who mock his prayers: "There is no one listening"
(Ps. 59:7). If this be Jerusalem, it is Jerusalem profaned—or rather
secularized, a city in history, where God is not in ready communication with man. The historical books of the Old Testament report
the recession of God's voice, from the thunder on Sinai to the silent
rubble of the books of Maccabees.

Yet the word of God continues to resound in the historical city.
It sounds in the many psalms which announce to all the world its
duty to praise Yahweh. The presence of God on Mount Zion is not
in thunder and cloud of light, but in the continuous theophany of a
faithful people's voiced celebration of their faithful God. Insisting
that his prayer rises to God each hour and each day, the psalmist
creates in his song a spoken covenant with God which is not past,
but present. It is a sign more enduring than the holy city and its
Temple, but as human speech it endures *through* time, not *beyond*
time like the heavenly Jerusalem. Psalm 89, for example, begins
with a conjunction of these two durations, human fidelity in word
and divine fidelity in his heavenly court:

I will celebrate your love for ever, Yahweh,
age after age my words shall proclaim your faithfulness;

for I claim that love is built to last for ever
and your faithfulness founded firmly in the heavens.

Ps. 89:1-2

Like the Temple, it can experience vicissitude. The volume of the song, the conviction and power of its singers, the attentiveness and response of those who hear, all may fluctuate through time.

The fragility and endurance of the word, proclaimed in the city, is the theme of the prophets. In each of the major prophets, the word of God enters dramatically into human time. It comes at a defined historical moment—"the year of King Uzziah's death" (Isaiah), "the thirteenth year of Josiah son of Amon" (Jeremiah), "the fifth year of exile for King Jehoiachin" (Ezekiel). Though accompanied by visions, the call of the prophet is a call to speak words, the words of God, dialectically opposed to the king's word, the words of a faction, or the words of the crowd. The Hebrew *nabi,* prophet, like its Greek-derived English equivalent, bespeaks the verbal nature of prophecy: he is the one called forth, who must proclaim the word, to call others out—call them out of the city's obstinate and inarticulate crowd.

For to the prophets there is little difference between Jerusalem and Babylon. Their word cannot be understood in either city; Babel's curse seems to have rebounded on the messenger of God. All the prophets represent themselves as wandering through a city which will not listen. Some of its people are preoccupied with the most immediate gratifications which the city provides: Jeremiah, roving through the streets, finds only deceit, debauchery, and violence (Jer. 5:6). Others, though they take a longer view, refer it just as simply to their own advantage. Isaiah condemns "those who add house to house / and join field to field / until everywhere belongs to them" (Isa. 5:8). Ezekiel's tour of the city reveals a welter of idols, a tumult of voices invoking Tammuz, Astarte, or the sun— any god whose favor might be more immediately palpable than Yahweh's. Both Isaiah and Jeremiah observe that the worship of the true God also has become an idolatry, undertaken for immediate and magical purposes.

The city's leaders, busy shoring up the city's walls and treaties, hear only sedition in the prophet's words. His message never comes in a good season, but always in the midst of crisis, and always saying exactly what a beleaguered city does *not* want to hear. Jeremiah is disputed, harassed and bullied by the city's own prophets, men of more sanguine expectation. The prophet of God is arrested and pitched into an oubliette; his words, as written on a scroll, are confiscated, judicially reviewed, and burnt in the brazier where the king warms his feet.

The prophet addresses a city that has met the silence of God in its own way, with prayers to more obliging gods and with the good news of hireling prophets. The legend of Babel reflects not only the multilingual quality of every real city, but also the incessant, self-congratulating, self-propelling racket of the City of Man. The purport of its din is "business as usual." Where can the word resound that would summon the faithful out of this city?

Despite the noise, despite the indifference and hostility, the prophet's business is in the city. He must carry God's word into the streets and into the courts and council rooms, in Jerusalem and Babylon alike. For the prophet there is no sanctuary at the city's heart where holiness remains untainted. When he goes up to the Temple, it is to bear witness that the shrine has been defiled, routinely, by the hypocritical worship of its own adherents. When he imagines a pure temple where God may be found, it stands at an apocalyptic distance. Still the prophet's cosmos has a center, founded not on walls and baldachins, but on the word of God. Oriented by that word, the prophet wanders through the city, matching his message against the city's din.

So the Gospel of Saint John renders the career of Christ. His first public act is a jeremiad against hypocritical worshipers in the Temple. But having ceremonially "cleansed" the Temple, Jesus announces that its religious role is ended; he, as the Word of God made flesh, is the new temple and center of faith. Unlike the synoptic evangelists, John presents Christ as a prophet who is at home in the city. His business there is discourse. He visits the Temple to discharge his ceremonial duties, but it serves him chiefly as a place in which to teach. It is a center, not because it is a building within a wall atop an acropolis within a fortified city, but because it is a place frequented by men and women to whom a prophet can address the words of life. In John's gospel, Jesus moves freely through the city, using his voice to heal, to admonish, to controvert. To those Jews preoccupied with preserving the sanctity of their city and of its Temple, Jesus appears as a demon, who must be expelled from the city; his voice is that of one diabolically possessed, a source and a sound of confusion.

John's Jerusalem too resounds with other voices. In its rooms the chief priests and the Pharisees conspire, Caiaphas and Pilate and the Sanhedrin conduct their interrogations and make their bargains. In its courts Judas betrays Christ and Peter renounces him. John renders Christ's interview with Pilate as a parley between God's city and man's over the power of words. Christ tries to turn the issue—are you a king?—from spatial territorial claims to the authority of his word:

> "Yes, I am a king. I was born for this, I came into the world for this: to bear witness to the truth; and all who are on the side of truth listen to my voice."
> "Truth?" said Pilate; "What is that?"   (John 18:37–38)

Perhaps this is the response of a weary bureaucrat in a country of fanatics, but it also expresses a view of language as profane, as having no vision of truth on which to center itself. Pilate's sophistication neutralizes the word's power to summon its hearer to belief. Turning from the single voice within the praetorium to the unanimous crowd outside, refusing later to recast the phrasing of his judgment, Pilate reveals a weariness with words that is far more deadening than the outrage of the Pharisees—which produced the convert zeal of Saint Paul.

And Paul's spoken testimony, significantly, proves least successful when in Athens he addresses the same skeptical Hellenism that had nurtured Pilate. Luke says of that city, "The one amusement the Athenians and the foreigners living there seem to have, apart from discussing the latest ideas, is listening to lectures about them" (Acts 17:21). They treat Paul's proclamation as one more such lecture; and find it sufficiently entertaining to invite him back for another session. Paul has told them "God has fixed a day when the whole world will be judged"; and they respond "We would like to hear you talk about this again." In an atmosphere enervated with intellectual novelties, the urgency of his proclamation is lost: there is always tomorrow, always time for another lecture and another viewpoint. Like Pilate, the Athenians are no longer seekers of truth. In a city where the vendors of ideas compete as hotly as the hucksters of chickpeas or of slave boys, words lose their absolute significance and become only the vehicles of fashion and of self-display.[1]

The City of Man, negating the word's power to incorporate those who hear it, trivializes the human diversity which every real city contains. To profane language is to destroy the power of each person to touch another in his being, in his sense of his own unique self. It is to undermine the power of words to join humans one to another, in either personal or civil association. This produces not diversity, but simple disparity.

A city of profaned words was what Saint Augustine found in Carthage when he came there as a young man from the simple village life of Tagaste. Though the crackle of "unholy loves" in that metropolis has captured most attention, Augustine's record of the city in the *Confessions* is more a depiction of an overwhelming hubbub of alternative philosophical beliefs, by which he was long confused and detained. The mature Augustine, oriented on the true word of God, in memory revisits Carthage to marvel, prophet-like, at the debasement of language there. As Socrates' foes in the *Gorgias* and in the *Republic* were the rhetoricians and sophists for whom an idea's truth was wholly secondary to its packaging and delivery, so the villains of Augustine's book are the rhetoricians who taught him words without value, and the academicians who professed ideas without belief—members of "a profession where those who deceive most people have the biggest reputations." Trained himself as a rhetorician and philosopher, he wrote several pamphlets "On the Beautiful and the Fitting," which retrospect reveals as one of the vanities that so long screened from him the real purpose of his life: "As I wrote them, my mind was filled with fantasies which made such a noise that the ears of my heart were deafened."[2] The schools where he teaches are continuously in tumult, the students entering and leaving at will, shouting at the teacher and at their fellow students. And the noise of urban pleasures fills the other hours and masks the silence in which one might seek truth, leading Augustine to the "lying" speeches of the theater and drawing his friend Alypius to join the crowd roaring for the gladiators in the circus.

When he flees Carthage to a less distracted life in Rome and later in Milan, Augustine meets the orthodox Catholic bishop Ambrose, to whom he is first drawn by his eloquence in preaching. Augustine, ever the rhetorician, so construes his autobiography as to make it not only a pilgrimage from one city to another, but also a flight from the multiplicity and contrariety of words, to the truth of the unitary Word of God. It is to Christ as incarnate Word, and to scripture as divine Word, that he is ultimately converted. Though recognizing at last his intellectual and moral errors, he nevertheless defers acting on this conviction, detained by other Carthaginian voices, those unholy loves, "pulling me by the garment of my flesh and softly murmuring in my ear" (8. 11). At last, in Milan, in an enclosed garden, he finds the space where the Word can speak above the noise.

Silent in his extremity of soul, he hears a voice. It is not the voice of God, but a providential coincidence of sound afforded by his urban setting: from another house comes the cry of a child repeating in a singsong, "Take it and read it." What he reads is a passage of scripture, Saint Paul to the Romans, an authoritative summons to awaken from the pleasures of the flesh: not an unfamiliar passage, since he has just been studying the epistles. But it strikes him now not as words, but as the undoubtable Word, "and all the shadows of my doubt were swept away" (8. 12). From the numbing homogeneity of profane words to the illumination of scripture, Augustine has moved out of the city's undifferentiated space into a momentarily sacred center. And from time profane he has awakened into a sense of time sacred. The decisive act of his life is made, and the *Confessions* has only a few more narrative events to tell before turning, in the last four chapters, to the mystery of God's word and its interventions into time. Voices, human and divine, have made Augustine's city holy—not by altering its arrangement in space, but by changing its orientation in time.

Early in the book Augustine marveled at how he had once gradually put aside his grief at the death of a close friend. "Time is no void," he observed; *non vacant tempora* (4. 8). The intellectual and physical pleasures of his life steadily reasserted themselves so as to fill all his time, leaving no gap to harbor sorrow. Now, towards his book's conclusion, he scrutinizes more closely the wonder of sacred time and the impossibility of comprehending it with a spatial image. What is that "beginning" of time, when God's word brought forth the heavens and the earth? What is "the present," in which

God always lives, but which is imperceptible to man? He pares "the present" down from years and months to an hour, a moment:

> If anything can be meant by a point of time so small that it cannot be divided into even the most minute particles of moments, that is the only time that can be called "present." And such a time must fly so rapidly from future to past that it has no duration and no extension. (11. 15)

Concluding that "the present has no space," he turns to a different medium for an image to give him some comprehension of time. This is the continuum of sound: the anticipation, speaking, and remembering of human utterance. From this image he passes to the creational word of God, which sustains realities in time, as the human voice sustains words. So conceived, time is sacred—not in the old cyclical way, but because it is open at every moment to the presence of God, as He inspires man, as man praises Him. Without such a key, time remains the "vacant," infinitely divisible, infinitely extensible homogeneous torrent of moments, in which all events—like Augustine's youthful sorrow—are quickly eroded. That is time without center, time profane, time in the City of Man. Composed of tightly linked moments, each with its own preoccupation, it is proof against that two-edged sword, God's word, which the prophet bears into the city.

Time, sacred and profane, and the word, sacred and profane, were the concerns of T. S. Eliot, who evidently took his role as that of prophet in the modern city. The dimensionless infinity of God may at any time break in on the linear infinity of profane time, giving a "still center" to the changing world, and a significance to history. The occupation of the saint, he says in *The Dry Salvages,* is "to apprehend / The point of intersection of the timeless / With time."[3] But man need not expose himself to such apprehensions. Searching the reaches of past and future, he can cling to a unidimensional world that allows for no intersections at all. In the fifth section of "Ash Wednesday" are quoted passages from the Good Friday service in which Christ speaks as the rejected and suffering servant of God's word. The poem then asks

> Where shall the word be found, where will the word
> Resound? Not here, there is not enough silence
> Not on the sea or on the islands, not
> On the mainland, in the desert or the rain land,

For those who walk in darkness
Both in the day time and in the night time
The right time and the right place are not here.[4]

Profane time has armed itself against ecstasy, against any summons from without. In *The Rock* he depicts London as "the timekept City," its schedules precluding interruptions from the sacred. It is a city full of the "knowledge of words, and ignorance of the Word." In *Burnt Norton* he describes the city's time, the interminable flow of uniform trivial moments, in the image of the London subway tube: "a place of disaffection / Time before and time after / In a dim light."[5] The *Four Quartets* proclaim everywhere the poet's dual problem: in the linear infinity of time, "the waste sad time / Stretching before and after," how shall the infinite Word find entry? and how shall authentic personal utterance of any kind be heard above the chatter and twitter of the city's noise?

Probably Eliot's most systematic treatment of the fate of words in the City of Man is *The Waste Land*. That poem is, explicitly, a recreation of the prophetic mode in modern times. It is a judgment unrelieved by any consolation. The poem's recording consciousness moves through the city—usually London, sometimes Munich or Paris or another modern metropolis—just as the scriptural prophets, and more recent prophets like Blake, wandered through Jerusalem, observing the residents' submission to Mammon. He records, as did Isaiah, the adding of house to house and field to field, with an attendant depreciation of the human soul; he observes the city's sexual obsessions, which to him, as to Jeremiah, Ezekiel, and Hosea, suggest a spiritual "infidelity." Though sometimes typified as the classical prophet Tiresias, the poem's speaker exercises a moral evaluation founded not on oracles or on second sight, but on his eschatological orientation in time. Over the cosmopolitans' chatter in the Munich Hofgarten, he lifts a prophetic cry that sees these vanities under the aspect of their final end:

What are the roots that clutch, what branches grow
Out of this stony rubbish? Son of man,
You cannot say, or guess, for you know only
A heap of broken images, where the sun beats,
And the dead tree gives no shelter.[6]

"I will show you fear," he says, "in a handful of dust." While a thoroughly urban poem in most of its settings, *The Waste Land* takes its title and many of its brief evocative passages from the imagery of the desert. As in the prophets, the present iniquitous city is juxtaposed to—virtually superimposed upon—the desert that will follow its destruction. "Hooded hordes swarming / Over endless plains," ruined city towers, the fall of London Bridge, seers vending deliverance, Hermann Hesse's somber view of eastern Europe on its drunken career to the abyss, all create an atmosphere of the Rome of Stilicho and Theodosius, when the barbarians are in the city, the aqueducts have run dry, and the dead seem to outnumber the living.

But the terror here is not political, is scarcely connected with the postwar confusion of Europe. Rather it is verbal. It is the city of European word-culture that lies in ruin. A babel of languages and of disembodied voices each repeating its own story, the poem reflects a society in which communication has been interdicted. In its texture of monologs and unanswered questions there is no conversation, no exchange of words. Of this verbal impotence the poem's speaker himself is the most dramatic example, for like Jeremiah, Jonah, and Hosea, this prophet testifies as much by the weakness of his personal self as by the authority of his prophetic word. He rebuffs with silence his wife's neurotic pleas for his attention and love. Her words—all words—are to him a summons into time; fearful of failure, fearful of risks, he consistently declines to respond, preserving his self-possession at all costs.

Eliot's later poem, "Ash Wednesday," helps explain his refusal, by developing the same theme in an explicitly religious way. To step into history with a decisive and authoritative word is to "redeem the time." But only the Godhead is capable of such an act: only the divine Word can intervene effectively among men, and usually even that Word goes unheard and unspoken. How then shall human words effect any redemption of time? "I am not worthy," says that poem's voice, repeating the Roman centurion of Matthew 8:8, but in a way that not only confesses the power of God's word, but disvalues all human words in comparison. From "Prufrock" to the *Quartets,* Eliot renders an image of man paralyzed by the insignificance of his time, the victim of an acedia that forbids him to act, to speak, or even to desire. "Between the emotion / And the response / Falls the Shadow," sigh the Hollow Men. In *The Waste Land* time is a centerless state of disaffection, a waste sad time stretching before and after. History, once the city's treasure, has become its unbearable and yet inescapable burden. The streets are full of whispering presences, Phoenician sailors and British Tommies, Cleopatra and Elizabeth. Trammeled in its historical analogues, every act seems to require a herculean reformulation of all the past. The future too has become intolerable. It is unimaginable, save as another trivial duplication of today. No one can project into it an image of altered condition. The city's false prophet, a fortuneteller called Mme. Sosostris, warns of death, advises routine and caution. The messianic "city over the mountains / Cracks and . . . bursts," becomes "Unreal." The prophet's personal history is a recollection of moments when he might have spoken, might have acted decisively, but did not. In the infinite flow of homogeneous moments, any one might be chosen for the utterance that would alter the future and give a center to his history. But no moment appears as special, as the one absolutely demanding action, and so he remains in his acedia, silent and spectatorial, as though outside of time, consumed with a sense of unworthiness and regret. Into the Waste Land comes no redeeming word of compassion or love. Voice, balked and unreciprocated, becomes merely noise, the sputtering of human engines amid the city's din of horns, motors, and phonograph records. Its incoherence (that is, its discontinuity) offers an image neither of eschatological time nor of a sacred present moment. Unable to imagine authentic speech, lacking faith in the word, the city cannot conceive of time as sacred— that is, open to redemption and moving toward a transforming end. Jerusalem, we are reminded late in the poem, has always killed its prophets. At the poem's very end, we hear thunder over the city. Three times it intrudes its "word" upon the desolation of the Waste Land: "DA." John of Patmos kept secret the thunder's words, but Eliot's prophet, following a fable in the Upanishads, interprets this protoword as three Sanskrit terms, "Datta" (Give), "Dayadhvam" (Sympathize), and "Damyata" (Control). Speaking a language antecedent to the Babylonian confusion of modern Europe, the thunder passes judgment on the desert-city through which the prophet and the reader have passed, a city in which are found no generosity, no sympathy, no discipline of self.

Insofar as *The Waste Land* is a socially directed poem, it reiterates the judgment of Jeremiah, accusing the city of following false gods, chiefly those worshiped by the sacrifice of life and by the objectification of sexuality, and of drowning out with its own confused noise the voices, human or divine, who would summon its residents to a less egocentric life. Eliot as prophet puts his city under threat of destruction both proximate and final, reminding his hearers of their city's eschatological destiny, of the engulfing desert—the Waste Land—that waits at the end of its allotted time.

But in the poem's conclusion, Eliot suggests that his city is not only the portrayal of a society, but also a macrocosmic image of the single soul. A footnote to the phrase "Dayadhvam" (Sympathize) quotes F. H. Bradley, the skeptical philosopher who was the subject of Eliot's doctoral dissertation:

> My external sensations are no less private to myself than are my thoughts or my feelings. In either case my experience falls within my own circle, a circle closed on the outside. . . . The whole world for each is peculiar and private to that soul.[7]

So the cityscape through which we have passed becomes the private interior world of the poem's speaker, his voice projecting his city only as a mental image in a sort of camera obscura.[8] The Waste Land is another city of the soul, like that in the *Psychomachia*. And like Prudentius's city it is fortified against intrusion, fearful of betrayal, skeptical of all that lies beyond it gates. Powers of silence and darkness—shall we call them sin?—have so invested this city that it cannot admit a redeeming theophany. What seemed an actual city, London, dissolves into a centerless congeries of individual citadels, at once fortresses and dungeons. Its citizens live in irreconcilable disparity. This is the City of Man, symbol of the Ego Absolute, both a collective and a personal aversion to the redemptive otherness of the word of God.

But Eliot's quotation from Bradley says that at the heart of this moral aversion lies a perceptual and imaginative incapacity: in a universe of profane words, man not only *will* not venture beyond his self, but he *can* not. Each person's world is unalterably private. One's vision of the city, however substantial it seems, is only a symbol of the self. Neither sensation nor word can penetrate the screen of appearances so as to communicate accurately with another consciousness. Experience is only the mirror of the self. Of course this is a perennial—and probably insoluble—problem in philosophy. At the same time, it is a spiritual problem most intensely felt in modern times. In the second part of *I and Thou,* turning from direct personal relationships to social connections, Martin Buber describes what Eliot has dramatized:

> Institutions know only the specimen, feelings only the "object"; neither knows the person, or mutual life. Neither of them knows the present: even the most up-to-date institutions know only the lifeless past that is over and done with, and even the most lasting feelings know only the flitting moment that has not yet come properly into being. Neither of them has access to real life. Institutions yield no public life, and feelings no personal life.
>
> That institutions yield no public life is realised by increasing numbers, realised with increasing distress: this is the starting-point of the seeking need of the age. That feelings yield no personal life is understood only by a few. For the most personal life of all seems to reside in feelings, and if, like the modern man, you have learned to concern yourself wholly with your own feelings, despair at their unreality will not easily instruct you in a better way—for despair is also an interesting feeling.[9]

This is Eliot's protagonist, solitary spectator in the theater of his own perceptions and feelings. Buber then declares that people cannot revitalize public life by dissolving institutions, or personal life by intensifying their feelings, but only by "first, their taking their stand in living mutual relation with a living Centre, and, second, their being in living mutual relation with each other." They must take their stand in a world coordinated by a sense of the sacred. For "Centre" refers, of course, to a spiritual reality, not to the magical geometry of some holy place. Like psalmist or prophet, Buber prescribes an orientation not on the temple but on prayer and on attentiveness for the divine word.

But the problem has a correlative in the physical reality of the city. Augustine found in the garden at Milan the momentary "still center" in space, where voice could be heard, to give a center to his own time. It has become a platitude to say of the modern city that it has no center whatsoever, that space there has been altogether profaned and neutralized. The gridiron is its mandala. It has neither garden nor agora nor shrine. This lack of imaginative focus has been analyzed in socio-psychological terms by Kevin Lynch in *The Image of the City* and *What Time Is This Place?* There Lynch describes the spiritual disorientation felt by people who live in a metropolis having neither defined limits and an orienting center, nor clear signals for both the passage and the duration of time. A resident of Los Angeles described that city: "It's as if you were going somewhere for a long time, and when you got there you discovered there was nothing there, after all."[10] Christian Norberg-Schulz, an architectural theoretician influenced both by Lynch and by Rudolph Schwarz (whose views on church structure we saw in chapter 2), enlarges on this:

> Technical means of communication have freed us from direct human contact, and an increasing number of people have become physically mobile. . . . A mobile world, which is not based on the repetition of similarities in connection with a stable system of places, would make human development impossible. . . . A mobile world would tie man to an "egocentric" stage, while a stable and structured world frees his intelligence. Nor would a mobile world allow for real human interaction. . . . Hans Sedlmayr has grasped the tendency at its very root, talking about "the lost centre." The environmental problem we are facing, therefore, is not of a technical, economical, social or political nature. It is a human problem, the problem of preserving man's identity.[11]

To discuss this problem, Norberg-Schulz distinguishes several ways of conceiving our orientation in space. Most pertinent among these are "perceptual space," "cognitive space," and "existential space." "Perceptual" is that defined by each person in his immediate experience. It orders phenomena as far and near, above and below, before and behind. It is "egocentric and varies continuously," a psychological horizon traveling with us as we move in space and time. It is the closed circle of which Bradley speaks in Eliot's poem. Cognitive space is that defined by scientists and mathematicians: infinite, homogeneous, independent of particular content or orientation, it provides man with a constant within which to explain variation and change in terms of empirically founded law.[12] Many modern architects and urban planners have translated this abstract space into an idiom of design, "building a Cartesian co-ordinate system with concrete materials." Norberg-Schulz criticizes such gridwork plans, saying they "satisfy only a small part of man's original need for orientation" because of their remoteness from actual experience and their failure to provide a ground for human identity and human interaction. The forms of architecture, the spaces of the city, were meant to be shared, but an architecture based on cognitive space can serve only as a graph on which to plot the disparate perceptual spaces of its occupants. Like Eliot's image of profane time, it allows for no intersections, it acknowledges no center.

Norberg-Schulz then argues for a third space, which he terms existential. He agrees with Heidegger, that to exist is to dwell, to be psychologically and spiritually integrated into one's environment, both physical and human. Existential space is founded on *centers,* not the fluctuating ego-center of perceptual space, but places of recurring importance to the person, usually "hallowed" through association with other people. Such centers are connected by commonly defined and significant *paths.* And together, centers and paths organize a *domain,* the territory known, as opposed to a relatively unfamiliar world beyond. These "schemata" give man an imaginative grasp on his environment, a "stable system of three-dimensional relations between meaningful objects" which allows him to discern continuity and significance within the endlessly dissolving perceptual space he occupies each moment, and to discover the points of congruence between his perceptions and those of his neighbors. These relationships might better be called *four-*dimensional, because they situate the individual in time as well: they make up a field within which experiences past and future can be located, and they are the fruit of psychological maturation. Acquired through human interaction, a sense of existential space aids further interaction. While a sense of perceptual space helps to develop the individual's personal identity, Norberg-Schulz concludes that "existential space makes him belong to a social and cultural totality." *The Waste Land's* characters admit they "can connect / nothing with nothing," neither organizing their own experiences nor sharing them with others. At one point in his passage through the city, Eliot's wanderer attends wistfully to the chatter and song of some fishmen lounging in a public bar, and to the "inexplicable splendour" of a nearby Wren church: shared and hallowed centers from which he feels excluded, as he is from authentic speech and action in time. A profane world, a city of noise without enduring centers, locks the individual in an egocentric prison of feelings and interdicts all significant human interaction.

The lost center, the silenced word, the sifting of trivial moments—these themes are dramatized with graphic immediacy in two now-classic films from the early 1960s, Federico Fellini's *La Dolce Vita* and Michelangelo Antonioni's *Eclipse.* Both directors, however, use their medium to juxtapose the profane space occupied by their fictional characters with spaces having a "hallowed" public, historical reality. Both take as their locale a city which for two and a quarter millennia has been a spiritual and psychological center for western man. All paths, of course, lead to Rome. The city is famous for its artful use of streets leading to secular and spiritual centers like the Coliseum, the Basilica of St. Peter, and the Tomb of Victor Emmanuel. And for how long the Roman *imperium,* temporal and ecclesiastical, served to define the familiar domain of western man! In Fellini's film Rome's existential space is set in tension with the unstabilized perceptual space occupied by its characters. Antonioni chooses an unfamiliar and geometrical Rome to complement the disoriented perceptions of his isolated heroine.[13]

Fellini's camera, recording the private decline and fall of the journalist Marcello Rubini, frequently records also the monumental architecture in which the shared religious and social values of Rome were once expressed. *La Dolce Vita* depends on the viewer's ability to "read" the settings in relationship to the fictional events which the film presents. Marcello serves in this film much as Eliot's protagonist does in *The Waste Land,* as an observer of the city's decadence, whose quest for personal meaning in life fails. A freelance journalist for the scandal tabloids, he cruises the cosmopolitan Via Veneto in search of material. But behind the sophisticates' frenetic motion stands the Rome of history, the Rome of shared and continuous physical and spiritual schemata accounting for one's existence in time and in eternity. To the actors the enduring bulk of an aqueduct, the Baths of Caracalla, St. Peter's, the Trevi Fountain are only props, virtually invisible. Of course they are not invisible to Fellini, whose vision, like Eliot's, is larger than that of the characters he has used to foreground his cityscapes. Fellini's film depends on the focal depth of his camera and his imagination and on the viewer's capacity to recognize and attach meaning to these landmarks of imperial and Christian Rome—on, in sum, our sharing with Fellini an existential space beyond that created by the film. He uses settings the way Eliot used quotations, to suggest an orienting source of shared value and disvalue, not dependent on the film alone, against which particular actions can be judged— existential space coordinating and connecting for the viewer the endlessly resolving perceptual sequences of Marcello's homeless odyssey.

Marcello's vocation is to fabricate publicity about entertainers, aristocrats, and their demimonde, stoking with his cheapened words the perpetual-motion machine of "stories" about "celebrities." In Marcello's world, noise has replaced voice. Television and tabloid journalism, in search of the sensational, intrude upon authentic human life. Pilgrimages, lovers' quarrels, bereaved mothers —the media mill gulps them down, shredding their existential continuity into "stories" and candid-camera "shots." Marcello's own attempts at personal communication are also never successful. Yet he takes for his hero an intellectual named Steiner, in whose home it seems that voices have created a shared existential space. There Marcello hears what passes for serious and intelligent conversation among the guests in Steiner's salon; there he hears too the words of familial love, for Steiner is as well a good husband and a doting and protective father. "Your home is a real sanctuary," Marcello says to him. It is a center, a place where paths come home; a still point where a man has anchored the small community of his personal domain.

But Steiner's sanctuary, and the faith Marcello invested in it, come finally to wreck. For it is grounded only on Steiner's own personality, and the intellectual proves to be Buber's "modern man" concerned wholly with the cultivation of private feelings—among them the feeling of despair. In their last conversation, confessing his fear that the peace he enjoys is only an appearance, and that the future may unleash some terrible destruction on his children, Steiner says "we should come to love one another outside of time, beyond time. Detached." Acting on this dark eschatology, this despair of the future, this sense of time irredeemable, he kills his two children and himself, leaving Marcello to drift bitterly in his own insignificance.

The city of *La Dolce Vita* is Rome. But, lying under omens of the apocalypse—beginning with a statue of Christ soaring over the city beneath a helicopter, ending with fishermen dragging ashore a great primitive fish out of the sea's abyss—the city Fellini has created is also Babylon. John of Patmos so called it, as did Augustine and Martin Luther. Another moralist from the provinces, Fellini's camera wanders through Babylon, noting its debauchery, its fear of time, its frenetic mobility, and its noisy disruption of shared existential spaces where truthful words might resound. Prophetlike, it measures all it sees against the historical cityscape of Rome, and against the need to be attentive for a voice beyond the tumult.

Eclipse, like *La Dolce Vita,* is a film about physical and psychological mobility. This mobility, though, is not measured prophetically against the monuments of Rome, nor is Antonioni interested in the social dimension of the events his camera records. He is not a moralist, and to separate his story from its cinematography is to reduce it to sentimentality. The film's narrative concerns a brief and unsatisfactory romance between a young stockbroker and a girl who works at translating. Piero lives by getting and spending: stocks, cars, time, love. Vittoria lives in indifference, an acedia of eros like that portrayed in *The Waste Land.* In her world there are no existential centers and so no paths; she wanders through a profane landscape of offices, apartments, and industrial and residential suburbs, locales which seldom repeat themselves. Lacking a domain, she is exiled forever in the beyond, the unfamiliar, the land without structure. The camera follows her wanderings, doggedly observing the spiritual vacuity of these scenes, recording how communication dies there, in monologs, in unanswered phones. Antonioni chooses to make the rendering of perceptual space his major theme, putting it in tension both with the cognitive space of modern architecture and with existential spaces near Vittoria which she may not enter.

One important sequence is set in her mother's apartment, another in the home of Piero's parents. The camera's inspection of furniture and decor reveals that these are *dwellings,* existential space imbued with memories and intangible psychological meanings. There are family photographs, of people now dead, standing before houses long forsaken; portraits of ancestors; heirlooms; odd sticks of furniture and items of bric-a-brac whose value is inexpressible outside the familiars of the household. But Vittoria finds herself terribly estranged in these dwellings. Viewing what was once her room, she can only say, "How I've changed!" The young woman who now perceives the room is not the girl who once existed there. The spaces are not the same, and she finds no continuity between them. In Piero's home, oppressed by its shadowy interiors, she gazes out a window, but what she sees only adds to her alienation. A church, a piazza, banks of tall houses sectioned into apartments. Across the way, an older woman comes to her window and looks out; on a terrace, a priest says his hours. Churchgoers and shoppers mingle on the square. Each figure is at home, or on its path. Antonioni's camera work enhances Vittoria's status as observer and outsider, capturing her fragmentary and unassimilating perception of the schemata in which others are living their lives. Her perceptual space and their existential spaces collide for a painful moment.

During their affair, Piero and Vittoria try to create their own existential space, not in old Rome but in the EUR section, a neutralized urban landscape of internationalist modern design in houses, squares, and streets. Partly Mussolini's essay at the *città ideale,* partly the site of the 1960 Olympics, partly planned urban disperal, a three-dimensional grid of geometric street blocks and rectangular facades, homogeneous and visually boundless, the EUR is the architectural equivalent to Norberg-Schulz's cognitive space. It has no Trevi Fountain, no Spanish Steps, no memories, no publicly given schemata. The lovers must create their own, by using words. "Do you see that stop sign over there?" Piero says; "When we reach that point, I'm going to kiss you." In uttering that sentence, he uses a sense of time very different from what he has displayed earlier in the film, when time was another of the commodities he sells, to be spent, invested, or wasted. Here a sense of the future is used to distinguish an object and to ritualize it by anticipation. He uses a tiny secular eschatology to create, for a moment, a center and a path to it. In the film's last narrative scene, they use the future-words again to define their own shared, four-dimensional space, promising to meet "Tonight. At eight o'clock. Same place." Their words seek to confer an enduring specialness upon the anonymous street corner and its stop sign.

But, having said these words, neither appears at their rendezvous. Their words, as attempts to intensify feeling, are—like Steiner's—doomed to fail. But the montage sequence that conveys this banal denouement dramatically translates it into an over-whelming cinematic effect in which all provisional human spaces are obliterated between the abstract landscape and the camera's perception. We see the EUR district in panorama, the square, the houses under construction, empty streets, balconies, scaffolding, shadows—a dozen objects which the film has taught us to associate with the two lovers. But they are not present. Strange faces pass. Buses pull up, but neither Piero nor Vittoria is aboard. The camera tears the scene apart, picking out details in closeups we can scarcely comprehend out of context: an eye, a wheel, a matchbox. The last image is a street light which fills the screen and then is eclipsed—by the black frames which are the film's conclusion, an absolute non-space which has finally devoured every kind of dimensional reality projected in the film. Like *The Waste Land, Eclipse* ends amid ruins, caused not by some barbarian holocaust, but by the camera's destruction of all existential constructs in which to set its images. Fellini's camera invoked Rome's existential space to pro-vide a context within which to judge his characters' uncoordinated actions. Antonioni's camera becomes one with his heroine's per-ceptions, an unoriented neutral vision at last dismantling even the existential space which the film itself has created.[14]

To the Old Testament prophets and to Saint John, Babylon was the place of profligacy, the city of decadence, "the mother of harlots and abominations of the earth." When these two films were new and sensational, it seemed that such was the city they depicted. The luxury, the revels, the lovemakings of a dissolute *bel mondo* appeared as the type of Babylonian excess. But to review them now is to see rather the Babylon of deprivation, the city on the plain of Shinar, where work on the tower stopped and men could not an-swer to one another; the Babylon whose inmost residents kept festi-val, not knowing that the outer city was already in the hands of the Medes and the Persians. The modern city is Babylon without its tower, a homogeneous grid in space and time. Its appropriate de-vices are the gridwork street plan and the grid of concrete and glass which in modern architecture passes for a facade. This is the "car-tesian" urban design which Lynch and Norberg-Schulz indict. Its lack of physical and spiritual centers contributes to the loneliness and anonymity of its citizens. Another critic of the modern city, Lewis Mumford, complains also how megalopolitan growth swallows villages and effaces old neighborhoods, thus obliterating the "social cells" of an organic human community.[15] A primary instrument of mass society, the featureless modern city undermines all the intermediate structures—neighborhoods, families, guilds, nationalities, churches—that might reinforce a man's compound grasp of his uniqueness and his community and thus might mediate between him and the social mass. Lacking such an imaginative sense of his domain, urban man must vacillate between Vittoria's dispirited isolation and Marcello's hapless absorption into the city's own vital processes.

In 1855 Walt Whitman proclaimed that the "word of the modern" would be "the word *En-Masse.*" All political boundaries, all social structures, all ideologies, were only temporary buffers which an immature humanity had set between the self and the cosmos, but as mankind came of age, these would fall away. "The whole theory of the universe is directed unerringly to one single individual"—a consciousness naked to all the world, absorbing it all, absorbed by it in turn. His poems celebrate Manhattan as a microcosm of that universe: it has no center, yet every citizen is its center. Through its streets Whitman floats as a particle of undifferentiated sensibility, now completely identifed with its being, now standing apart to "observe" and savor:

> Give me faces and streets—give me these phantoms incessant
> and endless along the trottoirs!
> Give me interminable eyes—give me women—give me comrades and lovers by the thousand!
> Let me see new ones every day—let me hold new ones by the
> hand every day!
> Give me such shows—give me the streets of Manhattan! . . .
> O such for me! O an intense life, full to repletion and varied!

Whitman's poetry, like Antonioni's concluding montage, enters a world of unstructured perception and perpetual motion—enters it with confidence, believing that the poet's own words have a magical power to sustain him against absorption into the mass: "My voice goes after what my eyes cannot reach, / With the twirl of my tongue I encompass worlds." This prophet of the modern needs no orienting summons from the word of God, for he and all men are divinities themselves. He puts the city under no apocalyptic judgment, for to him time is a boundless "procreant urge" in which man and his urban macrocosm dwell immortal:

> I do not talk of the beginning or the end.
> There . . . will never be any more perfection than there is now,
> Nor any more heaven or hell than there is now.[16]

But to even slightly less sanguine temperaments, such as Frank Lloyd Wright's, the featureless and crowded urban grid is not heaven democratized, but a graph of hell:

> Always the gridiron! Forever a bedlam of harsh, torturing shrieks and roars. This wasteful spasm of racing movement to and fro in the crisscross. Down erstwhile narrow old village lanes one is deep in dark shadows cast by distorted forces. Therein lurk the ambitions and frustrations of the human being urbanized out of scale with its own body. Here see defeat of all aspirations of the human heart. The sense of humane proportion lost. Incongruous mantrap of monstrous dimensions! Enormity devouring manhood[!] . . . Is this not Anti-Christ? The Moloch that knows no God but *more*?[17]

For Wright, as for Mumford, the alternative to Moloch is decentralization. *The Living City* proposes a centerless continental city, the population of America dispersed evenly over the whole land mass, each family with acreage of its own. Yet there is little real difference between Whitman's vision of the individual and that proffered by Wright and Mumford. Convinced that mankind is not about to go back to the parochialism of farm and village, the advocates of decentralization bind their garden city together with nets of vehicular and electronic communication. While this may relieve —or universalize—the problems of traffic and of overcrowding, such schemes do not affect that tendency of megalopolis, lamented by Mumford, celebrated by Whitman, to efface all intermediate structures that might stand as interpreters between the single soul and the universal city. Rather they extend the spiritual homogeneity of the gridded technopolis over larger areas of space. Whatever Wright's pieties about the sacredness of the family and Mumford's about New England townships, decentralization does not create existential space, does not bring persons together in living mutual relation. In Wright's continental city, the old city's face-to-face encounters are replaced by high-energy communication in the forms of rapid transit and electronic media. "There is now no advantage in a few blocks apart, over a mile or two or even ten," he writes. "Human thought itself long since rendered ubiquitous by printing, now by visible speech and movement, all but volatile: telegraph, telephone, radio, television, and safe flight."[18]

The volatilization of thought, the wrapping of the globe in a network of communication, the progress toward a global city in which one may be in contact with all: Wright is one of the romantic visionaries who, like Whitman in "Passage to India," behold the earth's "vast Rondure swimming in space," netted around with systems of human communication. Wright's city is confessedly a macrocosmic symbol, a model of the consciousness of posturban man: like Whitman's consciousness, it excludes nothing, it has room for everything that man has made; what is not found there does not exist. "It is the architecture of [man's] soul," he concludes.[19] He, Mumford, Buckminster Fuller, Teilhard de Chardin, and Marshall McLuhan all have sensed that man's great machine, the city, may respond to large doses of electric information as once the amino acids did, as Dr. Frankenstein's assemblage of materials does in the movies: may spring into organic life and consciousness. In Mumford's view, the city will move back from its nineteenth-century mechanical form, based on the dispersal of specialized activities more or less well coordinated, to a biological shape implying not so much organic function as neural propriosensation and self-consciousness. He concludes his magnum opus, *The City in History,* with a millenarian description of "the invisible city," the human nervous system extended to embrace the globe:

> Its mission is to put the highest concerns of man at the center of all his activities: to unite the scattered fragments of the human personality, turning artificially dismembered men . . . into complete human beings. . . . Before modern man can gain control over the forces that now threaten his very existence, he must resume possession of himself. . . . We must now conceive the city, accordingly, not primarily as a place of business or government, but as an essential organ for express-

ing and actualizing the new human personality—that of "One World Man." . . . For communication, the entire planet is becoming a village; and as a result, the smallest neighborhood or precinct must be planned as a working model of the larger world. Now it is not the will of a single deified ruler, but the individual and corporate will of its citizens, aiming at self-knowledge, self-government, and self-actualization, that must be embodied in the city.[20]

Here, as in the ancient holy city, we find the earth, the city, the precinct, and the single citizen aligned as isomorphs, each the model of the larger world. These visions of the postmodern metropolis are all implicitly religious, placing on the city a demand for spiritual fulfillment comparable to that which the psalmist once placed on Zion.

Mumford notes a dark side to this new organism, namely its susceptibility to manipulation by covert centralized authorities. In futurist or dystopian fiction the electronic city often becomes the nightmare city, a place of inescapable surveillance and of behavioral compulsions engineered by unseen managers, either malignant or benign: Huxley's *Brave New World,* Orwell's *1984,* Brunner's *The Squares of the City,* Burgess's *A Clockwork Orange.* Writing usually in defense of middle-class privacy and social autonomy, these writers invoke our primordial fears of unseen, demonic powers; but they attribute them no longer to agencies outside the city, but to a few technocrats at its "nerve centers." Beneath the city's apparently homogeneous power grid they discern a circuitry that leads to a single console. The centerless city has a secret, unimagined center, and there abides the horror.

Perhaps, though, a conspiracy of managers is not the only fall from grace possible in the city of electronic consciousness. Indeed there is something hopeful, or just simply old-fashioned, in conceiving this city as one more tyranny or oligarchy, in which at least a few individual spirits—the technocrats themselves, and usually a rebellious hero—continue to assert themselves. It seems more likely that the network itself will usurp the process of autonomous thought, leaving human beings only the contributory function of single nerve cells in the body's neural grid. Marshall McLuhan starts to analyze this in a passage in *Understanding Media,* but lapses into the old liberal paranoia about technocrat conspirators:

[The] power of technology to create its own world of demand is not independent of technology being first an extension of our own bodies and senses. . . . The need to use the senses that are available is as insistent as breathing—a fact that makes sense of the urge to keep radio and TV going more or less continuously. The urge to continuous use is quite independent of the "content" of public programs or of the private sense life, being testimony to the fact that technology is part of our bodies. Electric technology is directly related to our central nervous systems, so it is ridiculous to talk of "what the public wants" played over its own nerves. This question would be like asking people what sort of sights and sounds they would prefer around them in an urban metropolis! Once we have surrendered our senses and nervous systems to the private manipulation of those who would try to benefit from taking a lease on our eyes and ears and nerves, we don't really have any rights left.[21]

The brave new world of electronic consciousness is not a system of monitors summoning the thought police with their rubber truncheons or with drugs and soothing tape-recordings. Nor is it, as McLuhan concludes here, a simple collusion of politicians and advertisers. It is rather a world that has "tuned in." The essence of mass communication is not that it is centralized but that it is universally distributed. Civilization itself, after a labor of centuries, has produced a technical, economic, and social milieu in which the mass media—not their content, but their simple omnipresence—have become a necessary extension of the senses and a compensation for the accompanying loss of more immediate objects for the senses and the imagination. There are no plotters at a console, but rather a global conspiracy (literally, a breathing together) of newsmen in Algiers and Moscow, of disc jockeys in Detroit and Rio, of Bantu herdsmen and Montana cowboys with their talismanic transistor radios. In the psalmist's Jerusalem, human voices responded to the silence of God. But the global city is a city of noise only—of irresonant discourse, incessant speech that invites its hearers only to silence.

Whitman's prophecy of the "word of the modern" was entirely accurate: his "barbaric yawp over the roofs of the world" is not the speech of cooperative human conversation, but the celebration of a purely spectatorial self, addressed to a passive listener. Society en masse is a society of observers and listeners, bound not in any direct and immediate personal relationship but in their common posture—conditional and irresponsive—toward the instruments of mass communication. Unlike the old urban institutions, the theater, forum, market, and church, television does not create a sense of mutuality among all its viewers, but rather it multiplies millions of copies of one exclusive relationship, the individual and his receiver, its dramas enacted in the private theater of the nerves. An individual belongs to the mass, Gabriel Marcel said, when he finds not anxiety but reassurance in realizing that he is "just the same sort of person as everybody else."[22] The electronic citizen takes comfort in his awareness of the duplicative experiences of other viewers, readers, and listeners with whom he is passively incorporated as "audience."

Martin Buber describes the awareness of mass man when he discriminates "the individual" from "the person":

The *I* of the primary word *I-It* makes its appearance as individuality and becomes conscious of itself as subject (of experiencing and using).

The *I* of the primary word *I-Thou* makes its appearance as person and becomes conscious of itself as subjectivity (without a dependent genitive).

Individuality makes its appearance by being differentiated from other individualities.

A person makes his appearance by entering into relation with other persons.[23]

The citizen of Electropolis is not a slave, as Orwell thought, but an individual. Mass society is not built on ruthless suppression of individual action and opinion, but on fostering a cult of inauthentic individualism which flatters the citizen with a godlike sense of autonomy and self-determination, largely identified with his consumption of products: a cult of insular and negative "freedom" that is incompatible with choosing to enter into relation with other persons. The individual is free—to choose the content of the experiences he consumes, to use whatever persons and things are available to him for intensifying those experiences to their mechanical and physical limits. He is free to enlarge the radius of his perceptual space and to stock that space as richly as he can. But he is *not* free to respond, nor can he invite another participant into the experience enacted between the electronic medium and his own sensorium. He cannot redeem the time. He cannot help build a domain. Beyond the individuality implied by a choice of frequencies, there lies only the numbing homogeneity of being tuned in.

A few pages later in *I and Thou,* Buber describes the "I" as spoken by the demagogue, by Napoleon:

> He was for millions the demonic *Thou,* the *Thou* that does not respond, that responds to *Thou* with *It,* that does not respond genuinely in the personal sphere but responds only in his own sphere, his particular Cause, with his own deeds. This demonic *Thou,* to which no one can become *Thou,* is the elementary barrier of history, where the basic word of connexion loses its reality, its character of mutual action. . . . To him a thousand several relations lead, but from him none. He shares in no reality, but in him immeasurable share is taken as though in a reality. . . . The *I* that he utters and writes is the necessary subject for the sentences of his determinations and arrangements—no more and no less. It has no subjectivity, but it has also no self-consciousness concerned with its defined being, and thus all the more no illusion of the apparent self. "I am the clock, which exists, and does not know itself." [24]

Some have feared that the radio or television screen will project this demonic ego in its content, as the face and words of Big Brother. But in fact what Buber has described is the status and self-percept of the viewer, the media-consumer, in his relation to electronic consciousness. ("To me," said Whitman, "the converging objects of the universe perpetually flow.") Intersubjectivity is canceled, of course; and true self-consciousness also, annulled in the blur and noise of an audiovisual world. Napoleon acutely chose the clock, where time is made mechanical and circumscribed and set upon a plate for all to see. T. S. Eliot, in the predawn of the electronic era, chose the phonograph record, where voice becomes effacing sound:

> She turns and looks a moment in the glass,
> Hardly aware of her departed lover;
> Her brain allows one half-formed thought to pass:
> 'Well now that's done: and I'm glad it's over.'

When lovely woman stoops to folly and
Paces about her room again, alone,
She smoothes her hair with automatic hand,
And puts a record on the gramophone.[25]

The clangor of mass culture interposes itself between the idea and
the reality, between the emotion and the response: not just in physical sound, but as an insistent jangle within the mind. Whenever
words summon Eliot's hero out of his isolation, into commitment,
then the "sound of horns and motors," or a shred of popular song,
jam the frequencies of his imagination: "Is there nothing in your
head / But . . . that Shakespeherian Rag?"[26]

So too the narrative of John Dos Passos's *Manhattan Transfer* is interrupted by fragments of journalism, advertising slogans,
and popular song. At first these seem purely documentary inser-
tions, placing the action in its historical context, New York between 1897 and the mid-1920s. But at last they appear as the voice
of a superior and overweening consciousness which is subduing
and exploiting the psychic energy of the novel's characters, just as
the brain collectivizes the psychic energy of each of its cells. It is the
voice of New York City, which in those years was synthesized out
of several contiguous boroughs and cities. The novel's significant
action is not the petty strivings of its several characters, but the bio-
chemical process by which a mass society begins to think for itself.

This novel's hero, like *The Waste Land*'s, finds his own
thoughts crowded out by noise—not only actual machines but also
words reduced to the city's servomechanisms. Lacking Whitman's
faith in the stabilizing power of language, he feels his own perceptual space dissolving into the city's: he begins to experience reality
in the idiom of popular song, advertising, and tabloid journalism.

With every deep breath Herf breathed in rumble and grind
and painted phrases until he began to swell, felt himself stumbling big and vague, staggering like a pillar of smoke above
the April streets.[27]

As he absorbs the city, the city absorbs him. In a final hallucination
he envisions a skyscraper, jutting up through a rain of "nickel-
plated confetti" falling from typewriters, with a gold-foil image of
a Follies girl in every window. But there is no door to enter. Previously Dos Passos has implied that Manhattan has no center; now

Herf has found it. Previously he has called it Nineveh or Babylon; now Herf has attained its central mystery, its ziggurat, all surface and display, with no access to interiority, intimacy, or "depth." The seemingly inchoate modern city is poised for organization, for a leap to consentience and personality. It is ready to speak for itself.

The ancient city, Jerusalem or Babylon or Rome, felt a symbolic unity in its encircling wall, in its centering shrine, and in the person of its god-king. In imagination the citizens of Peking all could enter the Hall of Divine Harmony; in imagination the Aztecs ascended with their king the pyramid of Huitzilopochtli. Today the electronic city seems about to regain that spiritual unanimity—not in symbol or in imagination, but in blunt fact; not by the overt political force of Nebuchadnezzar, Moctezuma, or Hitler, but by the subtle power of political propaganda, mass entertainment, and consumption advertising. Such unification issues not from the centering and communalizing power of language, words spoken though time, grouping the citizens around a single shrine, but from the power of image consumption to divinize each citizen within his own perceptual space, dissolving time in the redundancies of recorded voice, videotaped motion, and manufactured news. Dos Passos carries forward the analysis of human psychological isolation given in Eliot's quotation from Bradley. Beyond the egoist satisfactions of its individuals, society is coalescing in a new form of unity. To Whitman this was a higher spiritual reality, but to Dos Passos it seems subhuman instead. As his novel ends, each of its characters appears, wrapped in worship of his own image, yet absorbed into the great city's own mounting self-awareness. ("Every one disintegrated," said Whitman of his companions on the Brooklyn ferryboat, "yet part of the scheme.")[28]

Manhattan Transfer, published in 1925, records the coming of age of tabloid journalism and the nativity of general radio broadcasting. Allen Ginsberg—an amalgam of Whitman and Jeremiah—extends the analysis of mass media and mass society into more recent times, writing in *Wichita Vortex Sutra* of the masscult packaging of the Vietnam War. Wichita has of itself few symbolic associations, but in Ginsberg's poem it becomes a "vortex" of telecommunicated images selling a colonial war. Listening to his car radio, reading headlines in the truckstops, Ginsberg plunges into this maelstrom of neon signs and electronic sound and print, armed—like Whitman—only with his poem, but knowing that words can mutiny or be sold out: the phrase "language language" often interrupts his quotations of public speech, indicating the point at which its words cease to summon up realities and begin instead to conceal them:

Put it this way in television language
Use the words
language, language:
"A bad guess"

Put it this way in headlines
Omaha World Herald—*Rusk Says Toughness*
Essential For Peace

. . . .

Has anyone looked in the eyes of the wounded?
Have we seen but paper faces, Life Magazine?
Are screaming faces made of dots,
electric dots on Television[?]

. . . .

conflicting language, language
proliferating in airwaves
filling the farmhouse ear, filling
the City Manager's head . . .[29]

In "Howl," a poem better known but less important than *Wichita Vortex Sutra,* Ginsberg identified this technocratic culture with New York and characterized it as Moloch, the Semitic god worshiped by human sacrifice. We have heard Frank Lloyd Wright too call the great city Moloch, proposing that democratic man flee from its clutches into a centerless continental city. Dos Passos's hero escapes from the City of Destruction into those hinterlands where America's romantics have always assumed that the preindustrial past still lived and organic personal life still flourished. Allen Ginsberg, in the depths of those hinterlands, finds that Moloch is close at hand. High-energy communication, the neural system of Wright's and Mumford's universal city, has overlaid Kansas with Manhattan, Washington, and Saigon. The city without a center has become *all* center, Babylon's debased words humming in the farmland air and humming too within Ginsberg's own head.

And so Ginsberg seeks to turn the global city into a disharmonic frequency within his own mind—interiorizing it as Eliot did London and Whitman Manhattan—and there to terminate the war with a healing mantra:

> I lift my voice aloud,
> make Mantra of American language now,
> pronounce the words beginning my own millennium,
> I here declare the end of the War![30]

Turning from the Babylon without to the heavenly city within brings him to a personal "millennium." But it is a millennium for the private sensibility only; it does not enter and transform history. Oriented only on his personal feeling of outrage, Ginsberg's word redeems his own time only; in Vietnam, he acknowledges, "the suffering [has] not yet ended." Of course, within his poem, the war is not over the soil of Vietnam but over the coercive power of language. His words attempt to set up an enclave of significance within which screaming faces are acknowledged as suffering human flesh, not electric dots on a television screen. But in any context larger than the poem, this private ascent to Jerusalem is another recognition that words have lost their communitarian power, another retreat to the world of atemporal magic like that which the primitive shrine-city represented. Ginsberg's declaration of peace is no more outrageous a proposition, within the poem, than is the beleaguered psalmist's retreat to Zion, or the aging Yeats's escape to "Byzantium"; but it *is* an outrageous consolation to offer, in the historical reality of 1967, to the tormented continental Wichita that is America. Allen Ginsberg, his mantra wrapping the world about himself, becomes one with the readers of *Life* magazine and with those on whose retinas the agonized face from Vietnam is transmitted as a sequence of dots.

Within the global city, or its visible nodes denominated London, Manhattan, and Wichita, a word *does* resound, but it is (in Buber's terms) the mechanized word of lifeless institutions, or the privatized word of personal feelings: *Life*'s word or Ginsberg's, in either case the word without a Thou. The electronic city of mass culture, seemingly neutralized and "profane," is an inversion of that eschatological holy city where the gates are never shut, where the nations come up, bringing their treasure and their wealth, and where the peoples who have lived in darkness at last come into a great light. There time, packed in Shakespeherian rags, loses the terrors of vacancy and silence, and the tears of history are effaced among columns of advertising. This New Babylon offers its own form of religious experience, the apotheosis of individual subjectivity, fostering a sense of individual autonomy and at the same time an indeterminate and abstract solidarity with the unseen millions who privately consume the same wafer of visible commodities, each alone and silent before the altar of his own sensorium.

The task of the prophet is to bear into the historical city the image of another city, the eschatological Jerusalem over the mountains. But if he is to bring a redemption in time as well as at the end of time, the prophet must also bring to the city the summoning word of God. That word can liberate those who hear him from the wish to make of their city a vain simulacrum of eternity. In the city God's voice is usually the human voice, lifted in the silence to address Another—God first and secondly the others who also call on His name. Those who share this common speech build within the metropolis their own domain—having perhaps a center in space, but always a living center; in time and beyond time, a personality grasped with the imagination of faith.

But the city is never silent; it speaks with a voice of its own, the voice of false prophets in Jerusalem, of sophists in Athens and Carthage, of gramophones and television in London and Wichita. Like the prophet's cry, the city's own voice summons the citizens to believe—but to believe in their common self-sufficiency and in the durability and satisfaction of the city's goods. Its call to worship is ultimately to self-worship. It masks the silence, it interdicts the call to Another. Where, in all this noise, can the word of God resound? The search of religious men, from David to Augustine to Eliot and Ginsberg, is to find that momentarily still center of the turning world, where another voice—not the echo of one's self—can enter time and redeem it, making sacred the city, where man lives in time.

5: Between Pentecost and Millennium

> *Ma certo poco pria, se ben discerno,*
> *Che venisse Colui che la gran preda*
> *Levò a Dite del cerchio superno,*
>
> *Da tutte parti l'alta valle feda*
> *Tremò sì, ch'io pensai che l'universo*
> *Sentisse amor, per lo qual è chi creda*
>
> *Più volte il mondo in Caos converso. . . .*
>
> *Inferno,* 12. 37–43.

RELIGIOUS MAN INSISTS THAT THE CITY, WHERE HE DWELLS IN time, should have a center. Not the old magical shrine within a wall, nor the basilica at the end of an imperial avenue; not even just the shared imaginative vision of a city beyond time. And certainly not the lonely, purely subjective egocenters fostered by mass culture. But where, in the mobile, featureless modern metropolis, can man found a "center" that is not subjective and yet not a monument to Moloch? In the word of God, as did the early Christians, a diaspora in the polytheistic cities of the Mediterranean world. In that word, as shared in a community of believers, there is a focus that exists not in space first, but in the varieties of time.

The Old Testament and the New both associate the city with egotism and arrogant human power. But the city has another symbolic valence in scripture, one relevant to the themes of personal communion and of spiritual process in time. This is, again, the symbol of speech, but not the prophet's public language of judgment and consolation, words separating the historical city from the holiness of God. Rather it is the personal language of love, which in Judeo-Christian scripture is almost invariably associated with

119

the city and with the message that the prophet delivers to God's people there. The prophet summons his people out of their unreflecting life in the present by reminding them that they are the subject of a narrative which God is writing in time, a story in which their relationship with Him continually changes in character and fluctuates in intensity as it moves toward its denouement. The prophets recurrently cast this story in the images of a comparable human emotion, a love story. The voice of God that speaks elsewhere with the authority of king or judge becomes instead that of the loving husband addressing Jerusalem, his bride.

As we have seen in earlier chapters, God's narrative in history is sometimes rendered as the annals of a throne city—a visual image; and Jerusalem is apostrophized as a single person because it can be summed up in the identity and deeds of its king. The alternative metaphor, however, is that of Jerusalem as a bride. This is an auditory metaphor, expressing both the fidelity and love of God and, more pertinently, the people's fidelity (or infidelity), in terms of a spoken promise. In Jeremiah, Ezekiel, and Hosea, God renews His covenant with the hesitating nation in the words of a marriage vow: "They shall be my people, and I will be their God."[1] The prophet, proclaiming the word of God in the streets of the city, seeks to recall Jerusalem, as symbol for the nation, to a covenant that involves the exchange of spoken marriage promises:

> When that day comes—it is Yahweh who speaks—
> she will call me, "My husband,"
> no longer will she call me, "My Baal."
> I will take the names of the Baals off her lips,
> their names shall never be uttered again.
>
> Hos. 2:18–19

"Baal"—master—applies alike to a feared husband and to the pagan gods. God's words here are not only a summons to return from idolatry, but also an invitation to pass from fear to love: from a God of judgment to a God in intimate communion with man. To Isaiah, Jerusalem in ruins is a widow, barren and desolate; his consolation of the city takes the form of a lover's call:

> For now your creator will be your husband,
> his name, Yahweh Sabaoth;

your redeemer will be the Holy One of Israel,
he is called the God of the whole earth.
Yes, like a forsaken wife, distressed in spirit,
Yahweh calls you back.
Does a man cast off the wife of his youth?
says your God.
I did forsake you for a brief moment,
but with great love will I take you back.

Isa. 54:5–7

Saint Paul renews for Christian use the image of God as the faithful husband of His people (Eph. 5:22–23), and in the visionary world of Revelation, all previous images of the city-bride are fused:

> I saw the holy city, and the new Jerusalem, coming down from God out of heaven, as beautiful as a bride all dressed for her husband. Then I heard a loud voice call from the throne, "You see this city? Here God lives among men. He will make his home among them; they shall be his people, and he will be their God; his name is God-with-them." (Rev. 21:2–3)

Like many of the symbols of Revelation, this image has no visual clarity at all, it being difficult to translate the beauty of a bride into that of a city, especially when both are entangled in the Tiffany confection of precious stones which immediately follows. Its power derives rather from its appeal to language, drawing together all the verbal patterns of the prophets' use of the city/woman image: John's words incorporate, within his own discourse, marital images from Isaiah and Ezekiel and the wedding formula found in Jeremiah and Hosea. It is not his intention to give the reader a technicolor picture of heaven, but to convey the understanding that these words, which God now speaks, include and conclude all the pleas and promises, all the lover's addresses, which He has made to "Jerusalem" throughout time. God's words, from alpha to omega, are fulfilled and simultaneously present in this symbolic city. The city where the word abides is (anagogically) the heavenly Jerusalem; it is (morally) the converted soul; it is (allegorically) the Church; it is also John's apocalypse itself, which seeks to culminate the sacred history of God among men not only by describing—and heralding—the last things, the end of the world of history, but also by weaving into his own vision the words in which that history was told. And, so, in scripture's final image of Jerusalem, the world of time is no more. Predication gives way to illumination; as in the entry to Abbot Suger's Gothic church, the word passes from sound to light. The endurance of God's word replaces the evanescing sequences of human speech.

But there is still one more chapter to Revelation. Throughout his book John has placed great emphasis on the need for fidelity to words, recording the repeated injunctions he receives from God to write down carefully what he sees and hears. The last chapter declares once more the accuracy of John's written account and invokes imprecations on anyone who might tamper with the text of his revelation. For he knows that the endurance of the word, in the City of God, must be balanced against the fragility of the word among the Christian faithful in Ephesus, Smyrna, Pergamum, and the other cities of Asia Minor where faith exists in the toils of history, subject to long cycles of ebb and flow; the apocalypse that culminates in the vision of a millennial city, radiant with the perfect light of God, began with prophetic exhortations to the churches in those seven cities, some complacent, some in confusion over doctrine or discipline, some suffering a loss of faith. The incarnate Word of God, though powerful to slay the kings of the earth and their armies (Rev. 19:14–21), is yet a word known only to Himself. The inspired human words in which John conveys the Word to his readers must be recurrently guaranteed and protected from tampering. And the word of God, as spoken by uninspired men and women in the cities of Asia, is more timebound still.

Therefore in his epilogue John descends from vision to prophecy, enacting the verbal functions of the prophet, to console ("Happy are those who treasure the prophetic message of this book") and to summon, by the power of the human word. In the visionary Jerusalem, only God speaks. But at the last, as we sink back into the processes of time, the city of voice is heard in loving dialogue, summons and response, between Christ and the community of the faithful.

> I, Jesus, have sent my angel to make these revelations to you for the sake of the churches. . . . The Spirit and the Bride say, "Come." Let everyone who listens answer, "Come." . . . The one who guarantees these revelations repeats his promise: I shall indeed be with you soon. Amen; come, Lord Jesus. (Rev. 22:16–17, 20)

In this dialogic exchange, "come" is the call both of Christ to his people, a summons to belief; and of the churches to Christ, a call for the Savior to return in his final glory. This image of the bride calling her beloved and called by him suggests a sense of urgency in time and renews the idea of fidelity to spoken promise drawn both from marriage and from the covenant of God with His people, applying it to the baptismal vows of the members of the Church. Such an image retrieves "church" from the architectural rigidity of the messianic Jerusalem and restores its personal and existential quality as the *ek-klesia,* the community of those singled out by their having answered the call of God.

Also, this image reformulates our understanding of the fourfold significance of "Jerusalem" propounded by medieval exegetes. As a spatial image, emphasizing architectural and political detail, the holy city seems most readily adapted to the "anagogical" triumph of Christ's kingdom at the end of time. It has proved less flexible as a "moral" image of the personal spiritual life and even more limited as an "allegorical" vehicle for the corporate life of Christ in his church. Further, this image severs the actual from the ideal, finding significance in the historical city only at those moments in time when its story corresponds to a figural event. In short, it is a symbol of uncertain value for rendering man's religious life in the Time Being. When auditory detail is added and emphasized, through the personal image of marriage, "Jerusalem" becomes less static and less statist. The metaphor of dialogue is more apt than that of politics for conveying the realities of spiritual life in time. It can convey variation in intensity, ranging from complete mutuality and communion to a sense of incompleteness or even absence; it suggests the role of human words in man's approach to the mystery of God; and it addresses the problem of conceiving the sacred as something both yet to come and now at hand. In the dimension of speech, several realities can occupy the same space: past, present, and future may all be grasped at once, through an imaginative act that might be called analogical.[2] In his version of the final judgment in Matthew 25, Christ seeks to formulate such an imagination, not for the exegesis of scripture but to inspire right saying and right acting during the Time Being: "In so far as you did this to one of the least of these brothers of mine, you did it to me." The epitome of the Good News—"the kingdom of God is at hand"—is phrased for an imagination that is at once expectant and fulfilled, both anagogical and analogical. And again, Christ's summons out of the crowd came only once in history, but it comes to the evangelized person now—comes, often enough, in the voice of silence—and remains, in the expectancy of his faithful, through time to its end.

In *The Meaning of the City,* Jacques Ellul employs this manifold sense of time in describing the Christian's life in the city:

> There is no means of retreating once the encounter with Christ has taken place. This is so not only because it is an act in the past, which nothing can change, but especially because that fact is continually changing the present, because no one can ever become absolute master of a present that has been modified by that past act. No doubt can be cast on the reality and actuality of that event, and its result is that the man who returns to the city is not the same who went out to see Jesus. . . . Never again can he enter the city with the same spirit, the same strength, the same submission, the same destiny. No longer does man belong to the city, exactly as he no longer belongs to the crowd, because his individuality has been affirmed by his encounter with Jesus Christ.[3]

Ellul's account of Christ's summons stresses the creation of a bond of intimacy between him and the single soul. His redeeming word exorcizes "the demonic *Thou,* the *Thou* that does not respond" (Buber's phrase, quoted in the preceding chapter), the power of the mass to render each of its atoms valueless and passive. Christ stands as the responsive Thou at the center of a thousand Thous. The encounter with him recovers a religious significance for the common experiences of man's urban life: "the awful mixture made by man is rearranged by grace and benevolence and by the Lord's act of accepting and gracing the chosen city with his presence."[4]

However, Ellul does not suggest that this focused awareness might, or should, affect the quality of relationship between the crowd's members. It does not weld them into a community. In his theology the Word makes all things new, perennially intersecting histories as once he did cosmic history, altering its dimensions forever. But this transfiguration occurs only in the "moral" city of the single soul, and anagogically on that day of fulfillment when God will bring to the resurrection that earthly city which man himself was never able to perfect. Ellul does not suggest that the words of faith, or the Word of God, might abide in the corporate life and speech of those who call on His name. Indeed, faith in Christ must unfit the believer for participation in any surrogate human relationship whatsoever. A community seeking to preserve the Word in its own shared words might reduce it to a formula which grows old and at last can change nothing.

Thus, it is appropriate—even necessary—that Ellul's exegesis of scripture and history should leap from Pentecost to millennium, for the intervening pages tell the dreary tale of the evolution and the vicissitudes of a corporate community among those who have answered the voice of Christ. That call is an eschatological summons out of time; but mediated through human words it becomes also a social communion inextricable from the time in and through which the words are said. The city of voice involves the dialogic relation, one with another, of those who have heard the Gospel and responded. Neither Isaiah nor John repudiated the city image when they took up the image of the bride to represent God's relationship with His faithful. Rather, they sought to accommodate them both in one complex figure. They did so to retain a sense of corporate, rather than purely private, communion with God.

Moreover, it should be significant, according to Ellul's own exegetical method, that more than half of the New Testament is the record of how the Word was shared, interpreted, misunderstood, and corrected over a span of just twenty-five or thirty years. This record indicates that carrying the Word into the cities of men was never—save in Saint Paul's conversion—a matter of single encounters with Christ, but rather a corporate activity inseparable from communitarian social forms within the cities of the Mediterranean world.

If the Acts of the Apostles is a history of the descent of the Spirit among men, it seems truly a descent, spiraling down from Pentecost to the Roman imprisonment of Saint Paul. Before Christ ascended into heaven from a mountain near Jerusalem, he directed his followers to return to the city. Luke uses that urban setting to realize the fulfillment of Isaiah's prophecy of the messianic Jerusalem, to which all the nations would come, going up to the Temple of the God of Jacob (Isa. 2:3). It is the season of Pentecost, a religious festival. The city is thronged with the people of many nations, both Palestinian and diaspora Jews, all attuned to the sacred character of Jerusalem as *axis mundi,* the goal of pilgrimage.

Within the city the Word lies still, concealed in a single room

—not the Holy of Holies on Zion, but a chamber profane in origin yet rendered sacred by the words uttered there some weeks before that spoke a new promise between God and man. When the Spirit enters this room, the effect is not to localize the sacred there, but rather to impel it out into the streets, making it public. For a time the city's multiplicity is annulled. Language itself gathers into a common tongue while Peter announces to the crowd the completion of all the promises and prophecies of scripture: "The whole House of Israel can be certain that God has made this Jesus whom you crucified both Lord and Christ" (Acts 2:36).

All the House of Israel, however, is not gathered into assent: to some this speech is only the babbling of a drunken fanatic. The Word can make holiness public, but—unlike the old, magical idea of the sacred—it cannot claim to incorporate the entire city as a single soul. Yet of those who hear, some listen and are baptized. And for them, the community of language passes into communitarianism in deed:

> These remained faithful to the teaching of the apostles, to the brotherhood, to the breaking of bread and to the prayers. The many miracles and signs worked through the apostles made a deep impression on everyone. The faithful all lived together and owned everything in common; they sold their goods and possessions and shared out the proceeds among themselves according to what each one needed. They went as a body to the Temple every day but met in their houses for the breaking of bread; they shared their food gladly and generously; they praised God and were looked up to by everyone. (Acts 2:42–47)

The first four chapters of Luke's account of the life of the Church insist that the call to belief in Christ has spiritual consequences that are not only personal but social. And these latter, communication and fraternal service, are not a repudiation of the city's ways, but a transvaluation of its secular ideals of shared discourse and cooperative enterprise. In Luke's description of the faithful, word and act are dual, addressed both to themselves and to their neighbors. Exhortation and prayer within the community, testimony without; distribution of goods by need within, healing without. And at their center not a shrine but the Eucharistic rite, where word and act are joined.

This depiction of total communitarianism is put at the beginning of Acts to convey not a chronological but a spiritual priority: it serves as an ideal against which the rest of the account can be measured. For thereafter the community's life is never presented in idealized terms, but rather (and without transition) in a realistic depiction of the internal and external difficulties of a group struggling to remain incorporated among themselves around the teaching of Christ, while seeking also to preserve their incorporation within the social structures of city, sect, and empire. Neither effort is represented as fully successful.

The breaking of bread—the Eucharist—establishes a new existential space within Jerusalem in the dimension of words rather than in the dimensions of temple and wall. The initial overlap of those sacred spaces, for the evangelized Jews, is immediately put under stress. The priests forbid Peter and John to proselytize in the Temple precincts. Stephen, arraigned for blasphemy, culminates his testimony with a prophetic attack on the Temple—"the Most High does not live in a house that human hands have made"—and is at once dragged out of the holy city and stoned. A general persecution follows. Many Christians flee the city, some to the hill country and some to Damascus and to Antioch, and the contrast between the Christians' situation in Jerusalem and their situation in Antioch provokes a reformulation of the relationship between the city and the sacred.

Jerusalem is itself a threat to the Christians' existential space. In that city the followers of Christ are only a sect, a "New Way," praying in the Temple and breaking bread in their own homes. And the Way is too much like the city's own cult to exist independently there. Their community, so close to the Temple, is magnetized by the old idea of the sacred which it represents. As the Epistle to the Hebrews acknowledges, the Temple draws back its own, and the Judeo-Christians' adherence to Mosaic practice renders them uneasy about the development of a gentile Christianity. In Jerusalem the Apostles are expected to conform to Mosaic rituals, though Peter has been assured in a vision that he is not bound, and though Paul has elsewhere preached absolution from the Law. Gentiles, forbidden entry to the Temple, find only half the sacred space of Judeo-Christianity open to them.

At the same time, if the Way is too much like Judaism for its own interior well-being, it is too little like Judaism for the city to incorporate it comfortably. And if it cannot be assimilated, it must be expelled. Though the Christian word occasions outrage in many cities, in Jerusalem the antagonism is most inflexible and enduring, beginning with the stoning of Stephen and ending, in this narrative, with an attempted assassination of Paul and with his arraignment before the Roman governor. (This is no mark of special "perversity" on the part of Jerusalem's citizens, but rather a biological incompatibility, the efforts of an organism to encyst and expel a parasitic organism within it. Such a reaction is inevitable when sect and majority are so closely related; thus Trotskyites were persecuted more diligently in Moscow in the 1930s than they were in New York or London.)

On the other hand, in Antioch, a great pagan city whose cult is alien to Jew and Christian alike, the followers of Christ are free to create a sacred space appropriate to themselves, one that can accommodate both Jewish schismatics and gentile converts from paganism. This accommodation, which long disturbs the Jerusalem Christians, makes it possible to distinguish clearly those who have heard the Word from those who have not. Luke remarks that it was in Antioch that the disciples were first called Christians. And it is the Antioch community that conceives the idea of general proselytizing —sending Saul and Barnabas on their first missionary journeys.

The success of these evangelists depends not only on the presence of Jewish communities in the cities of the Levant, but also on the form that Judaism took in the diaspora. Saul and Barnabas do not emulate Jonah, who simply entered the city's gate and proclaimed the word broadcast as he advanced through its streets. Rather they search out within the walls a subcommunity in which they can expect their message to be intelligible. They go to the synagogue, finding there not only a physical forum but also a shared existential space of tradition and value, centered like their own faith upon the spoken word, not the Temple. When such a space is lacking, as at Athens, the word often drops inert upon a ground of skepticism.

Their addresses to the synagogue begin by establishing the space they share, the space of an ancient story:

> Men of Israel, and fearers of God, listen! The God of our nation Israel chose our ancestors, and made our people great

when they were living as foreigners in Egypt; then by divine power he led them out, and for about forty years took care of them in the wilderness. (Acts 13:17–18)

Of course the speech that begins on common ground ends by dizzily enlarging it:

Now when David in his own time had served God's purposes he died; he was buried with his ancestors and has certainly experienced corruption. The one whom God has raised up, however, has not experienced corruption. My brothers, I want you to realise that it is through him that forgiveness of your sins is proclaimed. Through him justification from all sins which the Law of Moses was unable to justify is offered to every believer. (Acts 13:36–38)

Paul's sentences have led his listeners through a familiar story, but in the end they are caught up into a new sequence that leads to decision and to response. This response is either joy or outrage, bringing usually a schism within the Jewish community, a rupture of that very existential space that gave the Good News its original resonance. At the end, Paul is accurately indicted before the Roman governor as one who has stirred up trouble among Jews all over the world (Acts 24:5).

The significance of this "trouble," however, is rather different in the diaspora from what it was in Jerusalem. Paul's preaching occasions a split, like the mitosis of cells, between those who hear the ancient word of God and those who hear His new word; but both groups continue their individual existences within the accommodating body of the pagan city. Luke repeatedly represents the successful symbiotic incorporation of Christian groups into the cities of the empire, where the civil cult was quite distinct from the following of Christ. (And it was to be in those cities, in those synagogues, that Judaism would discover that it could survive, and prosper spiritually, when the Temple was again a ruin and Jerusalem again existed only in the imaginations of an exiled people.) Though the preaching of the Gospel occasions civil tumult in Lystra, in Philippi, in Thessalonika, and in Ephesus, the rioters are subdued by the civil authorities and the Apostles exonerated and delivered from confinement. Indeed, in Philippi they refuse a miraculous deliverance and remain in the shattered jail to receive a legal vindication of their rights. Such depictions serve an apologetic purpose, of course, in suggesting to the imperial authorities that Christians are not seditionists. But they also reveal that a clear disparity between the spirit of the city and that of its subcommunities makes it easier for the small group to achieve a sense of corporate identity and for the city to deal with the group in a context of common justice. The movement of Acts, therefore, is not only a descent from the unity of an ideal city to the multiplicity of real cities, but also a movement away from the architecture of a magnetic holy city, toward secular cities where the sacred exists only in the dimension of words.

The great theme of Acts is this development and uneasy incorporation of Christian communities as minorities within the Hellenistic cities; a lesser theme of that book, which becomes the major preoccupation of the Epistles, is the corporate identity of those communities in themselves. Acts depicts cities in which the power of the sacred did not produce unanimity; the Epistles reveal that the power of the Word did not produce unanimity even among those who shared it. The charismatic fullness of Pentecost gives way to the trafficking of Simon Magus and the deceptions of Ananias and Sapphira. The miraculous unity of speech departs, leaving the group divided into those who speak Hebrew and those who speak Greek, the latter complaining that their poor are not treated equally in the relief of their needs.

The Apostles respond to this complaint by setting up a board of seven deacons, all with Greek names. This act formally distinguishes the ministry of the word from the ministry of service, a momentous step involving concepts of hierarchy and specialization of function which could make the following of Christ an institution, a city within a city, eventually a city coextensive with a city. Most of the Epistles reflect the results of this decision. The pastoral Epistles, those to Timothy and Titus, concern themselves directly with the qualifications of bishops, deacons, presbyters, and "widows" (i.e., older women dedicated to the service of the community), all further specializations following from those made in the Church's earliest days. Liturgical practice and eventually architectural form were to develop from this division of the community by formalized roles.[5]

At best this stratification is based on a realistic recognition of differing degrees of commitment to service and to the teaching of Christ. (Though occasionally, especially regarding the status of women in the assembly, it reflects social traditions instead.) Therefore James's Epistle and Paul's to the Corinthians both denounce the churches for ranking the faithful by the standards of the city rather than by the standards of the Spirit:

> My brothers, do not try to combine faith in Jesus Christ, our glorified Lord, with the making of distinctions between classes of people. Now suppose a man comes into your [assembly], beautifully dressed and with a gold ring on, and at the same time a poor man comes in, in shabby clothes, and you take notice of the well-dressed man, and say, "Come this way to the best seats"; then you tell the poor man, "Stand over there" or "You can sit on the floor by my foot-rest." Can't you see that you have used two different standards in your mind, and turned yourselves into judges, and corrupt judges at that? (James 2:1–4)

At other times the Epistles try to counter this tendency toward specialization and stratification by developing organic metaphors for the ideal church, images which present the community not as an isomorph of the city having similar juridically defined roles and functions, but as a living body:

> There is a variety of gifts but always the same Spirit; there are all sorts of service to be done, but always to the same Lord; working in all sorts of different ways in different people, it is the same God who is working in all of them. The particular way in which the Spirit is given to each person is for a good purpose. . . . Just as a human body, though it is made up of many parts, is a single unit because all these parts, though many, make one body, so it is with Christ. In the one Spirit we were all baptised, Jews as well as Greeks, slaves as well as citizens, and one Spirit was given to us all to drink. (1 Cor. 12:4–7, 12–13)

Paul's corporate metaphor allows him to meet the question of hierarchy in a way that stresses service and cooperation rather than authority and jurisdiction:

> Now you together are Christ's body; but each of you is a different part of it. In the Church, God has given the first place

to apostles, the second to prophets, the third to teachers; after them, miracles, and after them the gift of healing; helpers, good leaders, those with many languages. (1 Cor. 12:27–28)

Corinth was a community troubled with doctrinal and disciplinary quarrels and suffering a crisis of leadership between evangelists and intellectuals. Paul's corporate image seeks to provide an ideal of tolerance, harmony, and self-incorporation for a group prone (like any city) to dissidence, to factionalism, to elitism and assertions of private advantage. In the conclusion of the Epistle to the Romans, he again resorts to an organic metaphor to encourage the responsible and appropriate participation of each member in the Church's corporate life: "all of us, in union with Christ, form one body, and as parts of it we belong to each other"(Rom. 12:5). In Ephesians this body unites Jew and Greek into one community; in Colossians too it is the symbol of the universal Church, Christ at its head. But the image was first developed to provide individual Christian communities with a way to articulate the ideal of their corporate identities—their existential space—within the profane space of the cities of the empire, and to phrase the ideal of each member's service in that corporate identity. Unlike the cities of Whitman, Wright, and Mumford, which evolve of themselves into consciousness, this organism depends for unity on the power of God, made manifest in Christ; unlike the cities described by Eliot, Dos Passos, and Ginsberg, it cannot disintegrate into an aggregation of private (albeit religious) feelings, for as parts of one body its members belong to each other. True institutional life and true personal life, said Martin Buber, can only be realized when persons group themselves in relationship to a living center.[6] The Epistles' image of the Church, as a body of diverse members with Christ as its head, seeks to represent the institutional ideal of a harmonious division of labor and at the same time to prevent religion from becoming only a system for intensifying the private feelings of its participants, a kind of higher egocentrism. Choosing a symbol in which the Church is not modeled as the isomorph of the city, Saint Paul and the other Apostles wish to recognize that the Church, like the city, is characterized by a diversity of roles and levels of commitment, without countenancing the city's propensity to rigidify forms and titles and to encourage its citizens in the pursuit of self-satisfaction.

The very existence of the Epistles attests the uncertain fate of the Word when it travels in the words of these apostles, prophets, teachers, and men of many languages. Each is a document written to check the instability of the Word as spoken in the communities of the early Church—communities then lacking established meeting places, licensed teachers, and a scrupulously protected holy book. It is fidelity to the Word that defines the audience for each of the Epistles, and yet each announces that the word has been imperfectly heard, hesitantly followed, or perversely flouted. Nevertheless, Saint Paul chooses for his *città ideale* not a smoothly functioning hierarchic institution, but a corporate body unified by voice. First of all, the Church is composed of those who have heard the invitation of Christ and who have in turn responded to it, calling on the name of the Lord. Further, each church is a community whose ideal is to be verbally at peace among its members and with those outside it (Eph. 4:29–32; Col. 4:5–6). Finally, each church is to Saint Paul a community whose spiritual life depends on the mutual upbuilding of faith through shared speech and through the Eucharistic proclamation of Christ's new covenant and sacrificial death:

> Sing the words and tunes of the psalms and hymns when you are together, and go on singing and chanting to the Lord in your hearts, so that always and everywhere you are giving thanks to God who is our Father in the name of our Lord Jesus Christ. (Eph. 5:19–20)

> Until the Lord comes, every time you eat this bread and drink this cup, you are proclaiming his death, and so anyone who eats the bread or drinks the cup of the Lord unworthily will be behaving unworthily towards the body and blood of the Lord. (1 Cor. 11:26–27)

The latter passage suggests an analogical imagination which apprehends the Lord now in the bread and wine, the paschal supper now in the table of the Eucharist, and the twelve disciples now in the *ekklesia*. However, for Saint Paul the dominant motif of the churches' shared speech is expectation, the projection of the community into eschatological time. His image of the faithful is recurrently one developed from Isaiah and from the parables of Christ, that of a party of city watchmen encouraging each other and keep-

ing awake as they await the dawn. "The Day of the Lord" is coming, paradoxically, "like a thief in the night" (1 Thess. 5:4–11;
Rom. 13:11–12). And First Corinthians, Paul's most encompassing account of the life of a Christian community, culminates in a
discussion of the Day of the Lord, Christ's *Parousia* and the resurrection of the faithful. For him the time is short; it rushes toward
its fulfillment in Christ, and the true function of words is to project
the imagination of each believer, and of the churches collectively,
into that day when Christ hands over the kingdom to the Father,
and when, as the trumpet sounds, in the twinkling of an eye, we
shall all experience the resurrection.

Toward the end of *I and Thou* Martin Buber generalizes the
religious problem dramatized in Acts and analyzed in the Epistles.
The infinite and eternal *Thou* of God, he says, cannot be set in a
context of space and time. But man, who *is* so defined, "desires a
continuity in space and time of possession of God." "Man's thirst
for continuity is unsatisfied by the life-rhythm of pure relation"; in
place of the risks of continally renewing the presentness of that relation, man secures God in time by making Him an object of faith.
Likewise, "man's thirst for continuity is unsatisfied by the life-
structure of pure relation"; in place of the solitary presence of man
before God, man secures Him in space by making Him the object
of a cult, "adjusting in a spatial context of great formative power
the living prayer, the immediate saying of the *Thou.*" And just as
faith may usurp the experience of relationship, so the communal
prayer may displace the personal prayer which it was intended to
support.[7]

However, says Buber, dimension-bound humanity must approach God through such transformations, for the same imagination that makes God an *It* can again discover Him as *Thou.* "Pure
relation can only be raised to constancy in space and time by being
embodied in the whole stuff of life. . . . Man can do justice to the
relation with God in which he has come to share only if he realises
God anew in the world according to his strength and to the measure
of each day." For an authentic religious imagination, God endures
through time "in the growth and rise of beings into *Thou,* that the
holy primary word makes itself heard in them all"; and He endures
in space "in the fact that men's relations with their true *Thou,* the

radial lines that proceed from all the points of the *I* to the Centre, form a circle. It is not the periphery, the community, that comes first, but the radii, the common quality of relation with the Centre." In his history of modern communitarian experiments, *Paths in Utopia,* Buber writes:

> It is precisely where a Settlement comes into being as the expression of real religious exaltation, and not merely as a precarious substitute for religion, and where it views its existence as the beginning of God's kingdom—that it usually proves its power of endurance.[8]

But this enduring relation with God is given to man, Buber says, "not . . . that he may concern himself with God but in order that he may confirm that there is meaning in the world."

> Only when these two arise—the binding up of time in a relational life of salvation and the binding up of space in the community that is made one by its Centre—and only so long as they exist, does there arise and exist, round about the invisible altar, a human cosmos with bounds and form, grasped with the spirit out of the universal stuff of the aeon, a world that is house and home, a dwelling for man in the universe.[9]

So Buber describes the four-dimensioned existential space of religious man, a space defined by its orientation on a centering Word and by the tissue of relation created in the loving words spoken personally by man to God and the words addressed mutually by the community to God and to each other.

Buber believes in a religious conception of space and time, founded in the word, that would not set between the sacred and the secular that unbreachable wall we observed, earlier, in architecturally defined versions of the holy city. Rudolf Schwarz, the theoretician of church building quoted in chapter 2, referred in passing to a religious imagination that could conceive "that man, sheltered in God, also has a home in the world."[10] Buber, speaking here of a cosmos that is "house and home, a dwelling for man in the universe," postulates too an imagination for which holiness is not referred to a reality beyond time, but discovered within secular, historical experience. This is an imagination of the word, spoken and heard. Somewhat earlier in *I and Thou* he wrote

I know nothing of a "world" and a "life in the world" that might separate a man from God. What is thus described is actually life with an alienated world of *It,* which experiences and uses. He who truly goes out to meet the world goes out also to God. . . . God comprises, but is not, the universe. So, too, God comprises, but is not, my Self. In view of the inadequacy of any language about this fact, I can say *Thou* in my language as each man can in his, in view of this *I* and *Thou* live, and dialogue and spirit and language (spirit's primal act), and the Word in eternity.[11]

Defined by its radii and not by its perimeter, a community founded on the Holy Word need not be the fortress of God. Buber is concerned with the danger that religious communities can become self-worshipful, defining themselves as a sacred space, while the "world outside" becomes profane, undifferentiated, deprived of imaginative reality. Buber returns to this danger in *Paths in Utopia*:

Wherever historical destiny had brought a group of men together in a common fold, there was room for the growth of a genuine community; and there was no need of an altar to the city deity in the midst when the citizens knew they were united round—and by—the Nameless. . . . The danger of seclusion might hang over the community, but the communal spirit banished it; for here this spirit flourished as nowhere else and broke windows for itself in the narrow walls, with a large view of people, mankind, and the world.[12]

The corresponding danger, of course, is what we saw in chapter 3: this thirst for continuity with the divine, dissatisfied with the fluctuations of pure relation, unable to accept a simply profane secular world, invests the *civitas* with the attributes of God. This subject preoccupies the later writings of W. H. Auden, to whom it seemed that the tragedy of the post-Reformation West was the rending apart of the medieval ideal of the "Sane City," into a transcendental Church and a profane State. His poem "Memorial for the City" is founded on the trope of a divided city, a "literal" reality of postwar Europe in which the poet read a psychological and civil allegory. The divided city, for Auden, symbolizes the fallen state of man, a divided consciousness: the principle of power and assertive idealism, called Spirit, has come to dominate and to deny man's Flesh, meaning his appetites, his moral and physical weakness, and his sense of humility therefor. In the poem Auden traces historically the accretion of the Spirit's power in the civil capitals of Europe, leading to World War II and the ruin and dismemberment of those cities that once had represented a humane unity of Spirit and Flesh. The last section of this poem lets "Our Weakness" speak in its own voice, concluding

> As for Metropolis, that too-great city; her delusions are not mine.
> Her speeches impress me little, her statistics less; to all who dwell on the public side of her mirrors resentments and no peace.
> At the place of my passion her photographers are gathered together; but I shall rise again to hear her judged.[13]

The last sentence draws into this allegory a Christological figure, identifying (as would Saint Paul) Christ with human flesh and human weakness, equating (as would Saint John) Metropolis with Babylon, and interpreting the triumph of the modern city-state as the crucifixion of Christ prolonged over seven centuries. Contemporary with "Memorial for the City" is Auden's "Horae Canonicae," a sequence of poems on man's life in the city, based on the course of Christian daily prayer known as the Canonical Hours.[14] These prayers extend an allegorical significance into the days of the week and the hours of the day. In Auden's meditation it is Friday, and the apex of the day is noon: the temporal world—that is, all man's action in history—is sacramentalized by its identification, for good or for ill, with the day and hour of Christ's execution. These poems rehearse again the paradox of the city's war on the Flesh. This war has, on the one hand, given man *"Fortitudo, Justicia, Nous"*—all his intellectual and ethical achievements—and on the other hand has led to the victimizing of the weak and to the rejection of the subconscious and its power to heal the psyche. The managers of the city, and the passive public, combine at noon to crucify the recognition of weakness: the flesh; the sensibility; the Word Made Flesh, who had compassion on the weak. Auden's sequence of prayers would require of the Christian imagination a continuous recognition of human weakness, a recognition implying both skeptical resistance to the city's own hubristic messianics, and also an imitation of Christ's healing compassion for the weakness of mortal flesh.

Auden stresses in these poems the imaginative passivity of the audience or public which a hypervisual mass society had created. He writes, in an essay, that the public "neither murders nor sacrifices itself; it looks on, or looks away, while the mob beats up a Negro or the police round up Jews for the gas ovens. . . . Among members of the Public, there is no contact. If two members of the public meet and speak to each other, the function of their words is not to convey meaning or arouse passion but to conceal by noise the silence and solitude of the void in which the Public exists."[15] Implicit in "Horae Canonicae" is the belief that in the Church's communal prayer, spoken words address the silence rather than conceal it and discover a Christological meaning in all of time. Auden's view of the city "redeems" the perceptible passage of daily time, somewhat as Augustine's eschatological city had revealed significance in the imperceptible passage of millennia. And his sequences seek further to raise to religious significance that long slack of Time Being which Augustine's exegesis of history left between Crucifixion and Parousia. The vision of "Horae Canonicae," grounded on the temporal processes of the day and of the city, uses the words of shared prayer to overlap the secular city with the Jerusalem in which Christ taught, healed, and died. In these poems, there is only one city, the "green world temporal," and prayer is an act of the analogical imagination seeking to heal the city's divisions.

What separates man from God, Buber said, is not "life in the world" but life "with an alienated world of *It,* which experiences and uses." The world of *It,* alienated from the spirit of *Thou,* is a world of unquestioned self-assertion and of power. It expresses itself in images of visualized space: it is a consciousness for which all realities are objects "over there," with which one relates according to the mechanics of relative power. To conceive the world in *Thou,* and in *It* illuminated by *Thou,* is not only to entertain an imaginative sympathy with all one experiences, but also to disavow relationships founded on power. It allows our weakness to speak and to address the weakness in others. Here again the imagination required is auditory. Speech, as a collaborative act of imagination, is not only a declaration of belief in the other, but also a mutual recognition that the other's person is in its depths forever a mystery which words can address but never define. Human dialogue, then, is a continuous and reciprocal confession of weakness and a volunteering of aid.[16]

Where the imagination fails, where the word falters, there is

Babylon, there is the city en masse. Gabriel Marcel, in *Man Against Mass Society,* locates its malaise in a set of mind that approaches the unknown not as *mystery* but as *problem.* The problem-solving self remains detached from what it considers, while in the recognition of mystery "I find myself committed as a whole man . . . ; we abolish that frontier between what lies in the self and what lies before the self."[17] While the psychology of problem setting has brought the modern world its great technical proficiency, Marcel observes, the same psychology extended into human relationships has produced much of the human degradation he associates with a mass urban society. The Nazi death camps are an anatomy of the state of mind fundamental to that society: the inability to approach, through imagination, the mystery of another's being; the reduction of persons to problems, upon whom a technical "solution" may be employed; and the systematic extirpation of relationships among the victims themselves.[18] Modern society subverts the human sense of intimacy, now by denying it, now by mass-producing it, and thus deprives man of any authentic focus of awareness. Mass man's insensitivity to others is balanced by an insensitivity to himself on any deep level.

For Marcel as for Norberg-Schulz and for Buber, then, the issue is one of touching the center. The key term is "focus," which is not only a visual metaphor (mass society has no sense of depth, of relative distances), but also a denoted reality present in French though lost in English: mass society has no hearth, no sacred place at its center. "Defocalizing" human awareness from what is near and intimately real, the communication and propaganda media of mass society set up fictitious centers of consciousness: Marcel, writing in the aftermath of World War II, speaks of the millennial kingdoms of Hitlerism and Marxism, though with more experience of the electronic era he might have recognized the instruments of communication themselves as the pseudocenters. Within the anonymous and irresonant mixture of mass society, Marcel proposes that religious human beings must set up authentic centers, communities based on the mutual recognition of another's personal mystery and on the mutual service of weakness.

The human creature under normal conditions finds his bearings in relation to other people, and also to physical objects, that are not only close to him in space but linked to him by a feeling of intimacy. Of this feeling of intimacy, I would say that in itself it tends to create a focus for human awareness. One might go farther and speak of a kind of constellation, at once material and spiritual, which under normal conditions assembles itself around each human being.

Each of us has a duty to multiply as much as possible around him the bonds between being and being, and also to fight as actively as possible against the kind of devouring anonymity that proliferates around us like a cancerous tissue.

There can be no authentic depth except where there can be real communion; but there will never be any real communion between individuals centered on themselves, and in consequence morbidly hardened, nor in the heart of the mass, within the mass-state. The very notion of intersubjectivity . . . presupposes a reciprocal openness between individuals without which no kind of spirituality is conceivable.[19]

In small groups—extended families and spiritual communities —which foster the intersubjective relationships of their members, some of the qualities of mass society may be nullified. However, Marcel does not propose these groups as a cure to the malaise of urban mass society. Like Auden and Ellul, he is skeptical of man's initiatives; like Buber, he believes that such groups draw their inspiration first from their center, not from their peripheral relationships:

It would be absurd . . . to suppose that there exists some technique, that is, some combination of methods which can be defined in abstract terms, by means of which we could reawaken love in souls that appear dead. Quite summarily, we have to say that such a reawakening can only be the work of grace, that is, of something which is at the opposite pole to any sort of technique.

It is only within very restricted groups, very small communities, that freedom can really be exercised in the service of grace.[20]

Only communities open to grace are, for Marcel, open to love, including the love of life itself, and to generous service.

Such a community, a "constellation" centered on a spiritual principle or person, leads its members into contingent faith in one another—a faith which, because it *is* contingent on that transcendent center, is open to doubt and to scrutiny. So long as that center endures, the relationship of the members may fluctuate in kind and in intensity, as Buber explains that even the best of human relationships must.[21] The church at Corinth—Greek or Jew, rich or poor, married or celibate, charismatic or not, partisans of Paul, Apollos, or Cephas—is yet one body whose head is Christ. In the existential space created by that Word, the Corinthians (enriched by the Spirit, says Paul, in all the gifts of language) may join in ecstatic prayer, or counsel one another, or quibble over variant theologies, or if necessary even judge a recalcitrant brother and exclude him from the fellowship of word and Eucharist.

Those with whom we are intimate are not problems "over there," but part of our own being, both extensions of it and limitations of it. In a context in which others are neither members of the crowd nor obstacles to be overcome, it is possible for persons to assume voluntarily the privilege of serving one another. Marcel's thought here is marred by an aristocratic conception of service as an occupation and as a determinant of lasting social hierarchies. However, he recognizes clearly that service is an attachment based on an acknowledgment of weakness—confessed by the one who takes service, and recognized by the one who tenders it. Immediately we have stepped out of the context of mass society and the City of Man, a world founded on the assertion of power and the obliteration of weakness. Once delivered from that world, as Saint Paul's epistles suggest, there is nothing permanent about the role of serving or the role of being served.

What Marcel, and Buber too, offer against the soul-blighting anomie of the modern *urbs,* is a renewal of Augustine's *civitas,* a community in time, bound in faith to one another through faith in a reality beyond time. Like Augustine's, their *civitas* would not be coextensive with any *urbs,* but would exist within the city, truly "in another dimension." Though likely residing in close physical proximity, the group would really inhabit the fourth dimension in which words are born, echo, and die: time, conceived as duration rather than as extension. In emphasizing an auditory and temporal dimension, this community is rather different from that which Augustine posed in basically visual and spatial terms, the *civitas peregrina,* wayfaring and alien in the city of man. Augustine's citizen fixes his gaze on a far-off heavenly city, God's kingdom at the end of time; he minimizes his awareness of the earthly city in which his lot is "temporarily" cast. In the city of voice, the word of God may enter at any moment, transforming His faithful and the world in which they dwell, but not bringing time to an end. To the analogical imagination, the *civitas terrena* discloses the kingdom.

Once admitted to the City of Dis, and having crossed the plain of tombs that lies inside, Dante and Virgil stand at the brink of that terraced abyss which is the antiform of Babylon's tower. Their path is there impeded by an immense fissure in the crater's lip, extending downward into the recesses of Hell. It was the earthquake at the death of Christ, Virgil explains, that so disfigured the symmetry of Satan's kingdom:

> A little while before
> He came to bear off Satan's captives
> From the outer ring of Hell,
>
> In all its depths this stinking pit
> Trembled so, I thought the universe
> Itself was pierced with love—a force,
>
> They say, that turns the world to Chaos.
>
> (*Inferno* 12. 37–43)

As a religious symbol, the city introduces into the welter of the profane world a focus for the imagination and a promise of transcendence. It becomes "the center of the world," its magical geometry of wall and shrine accommodating man to his universe, standing as its microcosm and as his macrocosm. In the midst of physical flux and spiritual inconstancy, it offers a promise of immortal life. These symbolic values have been discerned not just by primitive peoples, but by technically and culturally sophisticated societies in Asia, Europe, and the Americas, both those overtly theocratic in form and those that acknowledge only the laws of their own devising.

Though their sacred books acknowledge the power of this

magical image of the city, historicist religions like Judaism and Christianity have never been fully at ease with it because of its resistance to time, because it is a symbol of force rather than of love, and because it proposes an ethos and an ethic of self-contained and self-generated perfection antithetical to the sense of human mutuality and contingency proclaimed by their prophets and teachers. Dante can use the image only by inverting it: the center of the world is Hell's nadir. The power of love shatters the perfection of the City of Dis, theatening that contained and isomorphic universe with confusion and uncertainty. But in both Old and New Testaments, the heavenly Jerusalem appears as a dramatic—a climactic—image of transcendent holiness. How does its apocalyptic power sort with the heterogeneity of human life in time? Or, again, how may the actual city, that perennial symbol of man's collective life in history, incorporate a timebound sense of holiness? Is the *civitas terrena* to house two basilicas: one civil, the other ecclesial? Or must Babylon tolerate within itself a ghetto of resident aliens bound to a far-off celestial city?

Jeremiah advised the exiles from Jerusalem to build homes, to plant gardens, and to establish in Babylon the rituals of their common life. To Christians in the cities of the Mediterranean, the early evangelists proposed a community founded on word and act rather than on a holy city and its shrine. Though Christ is sometimes figured in Saint Paul's epistles as the cornerstone of a new temple, he is more often the head of an organic body, a body that has no interest either in encompassing the city or in assuming the city's static form. During the centuries called Christian, however, it was most often a forcibly baptized version of the old cosmological city that served the religious imagination, whether as a model of "the Church," or as the eschatological goal of a pilgrim people, or as the credential of some monarch's millennarian pretensions.

In the last two hundred years, though, important social and political changes may have invalidated the image of Christianopolis. First, the word "city" has now been applied to immense agglomerations of human life, high-density construction and communication systems, agglomerations so lacking in imaginative focus and promise of transcendence that they correspond to what the ancients would have regarded as profane nature. Second, civil governments in the mass state, for which Megalopolis is the overpowering synecdoche, have dissociated themselves from systems of justice and mercy that acknowledge any transcendent or divinely inspired ideals, committing themselves—with varying degrees of frankness—to a realpolitik founded on expediency and on the maximizing of power. The present condition of Judeo-Christian religious bodies has been accurately described by the German theologian Karl Rahner as that of a diaspora: the communities of the Word, Christian or Jewish, exist in the great cities of the modern, mass-society world almost as they existed in Corinth and Alexandria in the first century.[22] Though he regrets the loss of a common base of moral ideals on which to found the search for social justice, Rahner proposes his image of the new diaspora with a certain relief—"we Christians have no interest in maintaining Christian facades behind which no true Christianity is alive, and which serve only to compromise and to discredit such true Christianity."

In surrendering to the state the vision of the self-contained magical city, as a symbol worthy only of mass man's objectives, many Christians will share Rahner's relief. The general acceptance of his metaphor should dissolve forever old Charlemagne's dream of an earthly City of God, and authenticate Christian anarchism wherever religion still serves in any way as a prop of the state. Implied, too, in this surrender is a further, more affirmative possibility. The legacy of *The City of God*—a religious imagination altogether too divided between an anagogical holy city and a spiritually meaningless earthly city—might now be exchanged for that other imagination, equally religious, termed analogical: one that finds Jerusalem, old and new, within the secular, historical city, and proposes there to redeem the Time Being.

To redeem the time, but not by imposing on it some magical formula, remaking the city in the image of the heavenly Jerusalem, for such attempts have always brought the contrary result. Rudolf Schwarz, in *The Church Incarnate,* concludes:

> Church architecture is not cosmic mythology. . . . He who wishes to build a church needs no myth as his basis. . . . He must believe that God's son became man and wrought and suffered and he must believe that since that time there has been but one "sacred measure": not the Pythagorean number, not some magic spell, but rather the life of the Lord in body and in history.[23]

What Schwarz says of the structure of church buildings must likewise be the structure of churches in the new diaspora. Grounded on the historical incarnation of Christ, conceived imaginatively as the imitation of the Lord in body and in history, a Christian church seeks to extend his saving word and his healing acts into the historical city. But as the disciple of Christ, the church must share his human weakness. It must forsake political power. When Rahner modifies his concept of the diaspora by saying that "Christian ideas must be allowed to exert their due influence in the sphere of political life," he implies that Christianity still forms a political constituency sufficiently unified to negotiate with the civil order on a consensual "single common basis of ultimate moral convictions."[24] Today, though, such constituencies do not seem to exist. (If indeed they ever existed, as religious rather than as ethnic, regional, or class constituencies.) In Rahner's own Church, the pontificates of John XXIII and Paul VI largely canceled that allegorical imagination which focused the Catholic consciousness on Rome as on the earthly incarnation of the City of God. To propose a "church" speaking with a single voice in the political forum is to cast it again in the image of a holy city, magically girt and unanimous. Among Christians today there exists such divergence of opinion as to how the word of God might be manifested in the political order, that it would seem impossible for Christians to rescue the victims of the state by combining to change the state's laws.

Nor can the Time Being be redeemed by the Church's dallying once more with the power of the profane state. Indeed, the city of mass man, wrapped in its own millennial dream, insulated in its own noise, may be as remote from the secular reality of the earthly city as any pilgrim people on the road to the heavenly Jerusalem. Yet the mass state labors at a permanent process of self-redemption: part of its apparatus is a system of techniques for social rehabilitation. Christians, and even Christian communities, sometimes cooperate with, or even promote, the state's better-conceived programs. But these programs—even when motivated not by expediency but by some lingering concern for justice or mercy—are often uncertain in effect and inconsistent in the morality of their means. They all imply access to the state's enormous legal, economic, and bureaucratic power, power that no church has or should aspire to. And to the extent that a church formulates, sponsors, or administrates even the best-intentioned social program, it risks becoming just another urban institution, a bureau for the self-aggrandizing power of the City of Man, another agency through which the victims of mass society may be managed and oppressed. Techniques, said Gabriel Marcel, are the opposite of grace: one confronts problems, the other speaks to mystery. As an imitator of the Lord, a Christian can only address mass man locally and personally (that is to say, inefficiently), sharing his weakness and his suffering, not conceptualizing him as a "problem." A church's social action must be understood as Christ evidently understood his own curing of the sick: as a complement to his announcing the kingdom, an essential but secondary consequence of that announcement, secondary because inevitably selective and impermanent. Of all the sick at the Sheep Pool in Jerusalem, only two walked away cured, and only one—the one Christ touched—experienced spiritual regeneration. Lazarus raised must die again.

The Time Being can be redeemed only by a community that undertakes to live in time as Christ did, centered not on spatial models of timeless perfection, but on the word that summons into time; not on a program or an ideology, but on a religious exaltation, which, as Buber said, views its existence as the beginning of God's kingdom.[25] To live in such a community requires an imagination that is not only eschatological but also analogical, apprehending a religious significance in its own secular space and time. This is what Auden sought to describe in his later poems, this is what Marcel meant in speaking of communities that live in time but whose mainspring is joyous presentiment of an achievement outside of time. This is the imagination which Buber attributes to societies founded "on a response to the Thou made at its source":

> This act, strengthened by the similarly directed power of succeeding generations, creates in the spirit a special conception of the cosmos; only through this act is cosmos, an apprehended world, a world that is homely and houselike, man's dwelling in the world, made possible again and again. Only now can man, confident in his soul, build again and again, in a special conception of space, dwellings for God and dwellings for men, and fill swaying time with new hymns and songs, and shape the very community of men.[26]

Buber here traces the conditions of an existential space. His "special conception of space" establishes a sacral center, extends it to others as a common dwelling, and gives it endurance in the re-sounding of the word, "filling time with new hymns and songs." The response to the Thou, then, is twofold: first God's invitation and man's response, secondly the shared discourse and worship of those who make up the community. Withdraw either face of that condition and existential space vanishes into the alienated world of It, which experiences and uses. Sustain that condition and religious man may find himself delivered from the meaningless and egocen-tric mobility of the City of Man, may find himself the builder of dwellings in Babylon.

Such a community, then, is one attuned to the presence of God expressed through voice. Like the churches that Saint Paul ad-dressed, it exists in expectation of the fulfillment of God's word, in the kingdom. Unlike those churches, though, it understands that fulfillment as at once past, present, and yet to come: as achieved in Christ, as coming at the end of time, and as present in the daily ex-perience of the word within the community of believers. For some of them His word may come immediately, as a felt certainty of His presence; but for most it will come in a mediated form, through the shared confession of God's word in prayer and sacrament, or through the enactment of that word in reciprocated service among the faithful. In worship, this community may speak with one voice, addressing a transcendent center. Yet the circle with one center has an infinitude of chords and tangents: in speaking to the mystery of each person, the voice must recognize his uniqueness and recognize thus the diversity of the human community. Saint Paul's metaphor of the Christian body, encompassing a variety of ministries, di-rectly acknowledges the pluralism of the city as the old image of the cosmological city—Babylon, Atlantis, Rome—never could.

As the Apostles found, the word always extends itself beyond the boundaries of the community. Praise and service within the church issue in testimony and healing beyond its periphery. The analogical imagination summons into the present moment Christ's love for Jerusalem's weak and suffering. And the voice, confessing and recognizing individual human weakness, tenders his love—not to the city en masse, but to individuals, to families, to small groups, inviting them to dwell in that existential space where the word still resounds.

Such spaces once existed, to some degree, in the ethnically and religiously defined ghettoes and parishes that checkered the megalopolises of Europe and North America in the last two hundred years. In American literature one can sense that space dimly in fiction written by escapees from those ghettoes, notably in the work of Bernard Malamud, James T. Farrell, and James Baldwin. Because these enclaves were formed chiefly by external pressure and not first by the communal sense of their residents, the sense of existential space is an imperfect one, further obscured by the customary bitterness with which these writers recall and recreate the scenes of their youthful imprisonment. However, as these enclaves lose their coercive nature, they may be the setting in which genuine communities can be founded, by choice. Belatedly recognizing that the tabula-rasa, eye-in-the-sky approach to urban redevelopment has yielded human conjunction without human community, the agencies of the mass state are now looking nostalgically back at the enclaves they have destroyed and exploring how to renew communal identity in those that still linger.

That sense of identity was in great measure created by their religious associations—Protestant in the black ghettoes, Jewish or Roman Catholic in the white—and it may be that community cannot be restored there without some comparable religious renewal. Of course, such new religious associations would have to be as free of social compulsion as the enclaves themselves. Concluding his essay on the Christian diaspora, Karl Rahner anticipates "the emergence of genuine new communities" grounded not on social tradition and compulsion but on their members' active sense of spiritual brotherhood, fostered by the bond of liturgy and "the attitude of neighbourliness." This describes a community that continues to occupy ground, its members living in some physical proximity to one another. It is neither a "floating parish," nor a church which assembles its members once a week from all the city's neighborhoods and suburbs. If its center is Christ, its path the pilgrim way, and its domain the kingdom of God, nevertheless its center is also a church building where the faithful assemble both for worship and to address jointly the cares of this world; its path is the streets of their habitual passage; and its domain is a single neighborhood for whose care they believe themselves responsible.

To develop such a community is not to yearn for the old protective ghetto. Entered now voluntarily, it is sustained at a measurable personal cost: inferior education for the children, stagnating or depreciating property values, risks to physical safety, unbeautiful surroundings, a share in the city's sense of helplessness. Further, unlike the old ethnic ghettos, it cannot occupy *all* the ground, and so homogenize its residents, but rests its existential space on whatever human diversity its neighborhood can sustain. Finally, though its first compassion is for its own members, neither common prayer nor mutual help can be confined to that membership, but must extend into the whole neighborhood, ministering to those citizens anonymized and defocalized by the forces of mass society. Rahner concludes with another call for an imagination that does not merely sojourn in Babylon, but dwells there, building a place of hospitality:

> It will be necessary to construct far clearer and more convincing concrete prototype examples than hitherto of what the way of life and social patterns of such communities must be in order for the men of today to feel immediately at home in them. These examples must include preaching, confession, liturgy, work for neighbours in the parish, the charity of the community as a whole.[27]

Rahner's language, though, is here somewhat at odds with his purpose: those committed to such communities should figure themselves as imitators of Christ and of the first generation of Christians, not as constructors of prototypes.

Indeed, to speak of prototypes may be to distinguish the actual from the ideal, as did the cosmic mandala-city, and to set for the religious imagination the task of imposing one upon the other. The mandala, said Jung, is the product of an inability in the conscious life to overcome one's sense of psychic helplessness. An analogical imagination, surrendering to the grace of God, might not need to recoil from the city's reality into the formulation of ideal cities where holiness abides unpolluted by time and by human diversity.[28] The power of love, said Dante, shatters the formal perfection of the kingdom of force. In the analogical imagination, the kingdom of God begins here, in the historical city, which is also old Jerusalem, and new.

Why in the city? Not, finally, out of a sense of mission. As

Marcel said, it would be absurd for Christians to suppose themselves in possession of some technique that could accomplish the
redemption of mass society by reawakening love in souls that appear dead. The malaise is too great, the ministrants too few and too
weak. If the cities survive, if mass man is to be saved from the society he has created, if the time is redeemed, it will be (as Marcel and
Ellul both insist) the work of grace rather than the work of a program, even a religiously motivated program. And no seemingly religious mission founded on a sense of program is likely itself to
survive.

Why then in the city? Because that is where man lives most
fully in the complexity of human time. Christ's summons into time
is a summons out of mass society, but not a call to repudiate the city.
The countryside has long been the setting for spiritual experience
that is solitary and illuminist in kind, but the city is the proper ma-
trix for communitarian religions with a historically defined belief
that is transmitted through the fluctuating invitations of the human
voice. Within the diversity, confusion, and suffering of the earthly
 city, an indwelling church can become a center where the word of
love resounds, the anchor of an existential space: the light of the
world, a city on a hill.

Three-dimensional objects, like the "city" conceived simply
in space, enter the world of the spirit only through metaphor, often
achieving their effect by the evident disparity between real cities
and the symbolic holy city. The *civitas* of voice, however, is one
wedded to time, through the sequence of words, and yet one in
which the word can summon into simultaneous analogical presence
Jerusalem, Rome, London—now not "unreal," but as real as the
communal voices in them can make them, in the praise of God and
the service of His little ones. Conceived in voice and time rather
than in a special visual space, the holy city is thrust out of
"symbol" into "reality." In this way a religious community can become a presence of holiness within real cities, rather than the symbolic projection of otherworldly holiness upon the secular image of
a city. From his visionary New Jerusalem, John of Patmos returns
to his listeners in their communities of speech in Pergamum, Sar-
dis, and Laodicea. From being the "center" of a symbolic geography, the holy city passes into the temporal world of shared voice,
where the center is the shared existential space of a community, a

"church." And around that center lies not the confusion of the elements or the warring nations, but egocentric space absolutized, a mass urban society worshiping power and noise. There the kingdom of God begins, addressing human persons one by one, each in love, each in his personal mystery, each in his weakness, each in that silence where the Word reaches out.

Notes

1. THE CITY AT THE CENTER OF THE WORLD

1. Mircea Eliade, *Patterns in Comparative Religion,* trans. Rosemary Sheed (1958; reprint ed., Cleveland: World Publishing Co., 1963), p. 371.

2. Nigel Cameron and Brian Brake, *Peking: A Tale of Three Cities* (New York: Harper & Row, 1965), p. 119.

3. Miguel León-Portilla, *Aztec Thought and Culture,* trans. Jack Emory Davis (Norman, Okla.: University of Oklahoma Press, 1963), p. 46; Benjamin Keen, *The Aztec Image in Western Thought* (New Brunswick, N.J.: Rutgers University Press, 1971), p. 11; George C. Vaillant, *Aztecs of Mexico* (Garden City, N.Y.: Doubleday, Doran & Co., 1941), p. 171. While at variance in the assignment of gods and significances, all agree on the five-part world.

4. Laurette Séjourné, *Burning Water: Thought and Religion in Ancient Mexico,* trans. Irene Nicholson (London: Thames & Hudson, 1957), p. 89.

5. Eliade, *Patterns in Comparative Religion,* pp. 372–373; C. G. Jung, *The Archetypes and the Collective Unconscious,* 2nd ed., *The Collected Works of C. G. Jung,* vol. 9, trans. R. F. C. Hull (London: Routledge & Kegan Paul, 1969), pp. 310, 356, 360–361, 387–390.

6. C. G. Jung, *Psychology and Alchemy,* trans. R. F. C. Hull, Bollingen Series XX, 2nd ed. (Princeton, N.J.: Princeton University Press, 1968), pp. 124, 183.

7. Ps. 46:5–7. Throughout this work all quotations from the Old and the New Testaments are from *The Jerusalem Bible* (New York: Doubleday & Co., 1966).

8. The folkloric success stories of Daniel, and of Mordecai in the Book of Esther, confuse the issue by depicting Jews attaining immense prestige in the administration of foreign cities. The dramatic crisis of each book, however, is provided by the hero's decision to identify himself as Jew rather than as an unquestioning servant of the state. Within the stories' melodramatic crises and happy endings is the essential struggle of an exiled people, an unassimilated subject population. Thus such tales, though folkloric, are ultimately true. Not all the Jews returned to Palestine when an edict from Cyrus ended their enforced stay in Babylon; a prosperous Jewish community survived there as an identifiable body until the Middle Ages.

9. Though this chapter was written before I had read Christian Norberg-Schulz's *Existence, Space and Architecture* (New York: Praeger, Inc., 1971), his discussion of shared "space schemata" led me to revise some terminology to emphasize this point. See pp. 22–23 of his book.

10. N. D. Fustel de Coulanges, *The Ancient City,* trans. Willard Small (Boston: Lothrop, Lee & Shepard, 1873), pp. 259–261.

11. Lidia Storoni Mazzolani notes the existence of a corresponding Roman apocalyptic tradition, founded on oracles, legends, and cultural fears of a cataclysmic invasion from the east (often the Parthians), or of a rival empire in the east (often centered at Jerusalem). She conjectures that, while the official literature of Rome was occupied with dismissing these fears, they must have represented a real hope for radical upheaval among the oppressed plebeians of Italy. As the later empire became a symbol not of justice but of coercion to more and more of its residents, the apocalyptic promise of Revelation must have appealed strongly to the imaginations of the oppressed. See her *The Idea of the City in Roman Thought,* trans. S. O'Donnell (Bloomington and London: Indiana University Press, 1970), chs. 9, 10, 12.

12. C. S. Lewis, in *The Allegory of Love* (1936; reprint ed., New York: Oxford University Press, 1958), pp. 58–64, describes the origin of allegory in the personifications—Fame, War, Death—common to Roman literature, and connects it with the rise, during the empire, of a new conception of the moral life, Stoic or Christian: that of an internal conflict between the forces of a divided will—the *bellum intestinum* or *psychomachia.* "On the one hand, the gods sink into personifications; on the other, a widespread moral revolution forces men to personify their passions."

13. *Prudentius,* with a translation by H. J. Thomson (Cambridge, Mass.: Harvard University Press, 1949), vol. 1. The translation here is mine, not Thomson's.

2. HEAVENLY CITY, EARTHLY CITY

1. Saint Augustine, *The City of God,* trans. Gerald G. Walsh, S.J., Demetrius B. Zema, S.J., Grace Monahan, O.S.U., and Daniel J. Honan (New York: Fathers of the Church, Inc., 1950-54). The translations of Augustine are mainly theirs, though occasionally I have amended them to make a point clearer. The citations are given to the books and sections of Augustine's work, rather than to the volume and page of this translation.

2. Saint Jerome, Augustine's contemporary, uses these words interchangeably, referring to Sodom—and to Jerusalem—as both *urbs* and *civitas,* whether the context is physical or spiritual.

3. Educated as a hostage in the Roman Imperial court, Alaric was well attuned to the significance which Mediterranean culture gave a city. He had once ransomed Athens for the privilege of behaving as her citizen—for the right to walk her streets and visit the Parthenon, to hear the *Timaeus* read, and to attend a play of Aeschylus. There was nothing "barbarian" about his descent on Rome; it was instead the use of a native Roman idiom.

4. *The City of God* 20. 11. My translation of the last phrase. *Castrum,* Augustine's and also Jerome's term, does indeed translate John's παρεμβολή, a military stronghold.

5. The intermediary between John and Augustine is Tyconius, who in a commentary on Revelation developed the image of "two cities, one of God and one of the Devil, . . . one serving the world and one serving Christ." See Heinrich Scholz, *Glaube und Unglaube in der Weltgeschichte* (Leipzig: J. C. Hinrich'sche Buchhandlung, 1911), pp. 78-79. In *The Idea of the City in Roman Thought,* Lidia Storoni Mazzolani discusses many of the antecedents among Hellenistic Ro-

man writers of Augustine's antithesis of a "heavenly" city and an "earthly" city, e.g., Seneca (*On Leisure*), Cicero (*On the Republic*), and Philo of Alexandria (*On the Creation*). These are conceived, though, as a "greater" and a "lesser" citizenship, which may be held simultaneously—not as radically opposed orientations of the moral life.

6. Note that his theory of language parallels his moral theory, setting external relation against self-containment. See also 17. 3.

7. Erich Auerbach, *Mimesis: The Representation of Reality in Western Literature,* trans. Willard Trask (1953; reprint ed., Garden City, N.Y.: Doubleday & Co., 1957), p. 66.

8. *The City of God* 1. 35. Augustine develops here the pun linking the Christian "sacrament" with the Roman *sacramentum,* a soldier's oath of allegiance to the emperor, affirming obedience to the death.

9. Lidia Storoni Mazzolani remarks: "If the paganism of the later Empire concealed lofty spiritual aspirations—at least for a restricted circle—behind the thin veil of symbolic rites and mysteries; if it included the hope of eternal life, the yearning toward monotheism, the elevated moral teachings of Orphism and Mithraism, Augustine pretends not to know about it. . . . Augustine prefers to mock at the divinities worshipped by the lower classes, or to deplore the obscenity of certain rites which enlightened pagans, in fact, disliked as much as he did" (*The Idea of the City,* p. 273). In books 8 and 10, Augustine does in fact give a hearing to classical philosophy, primarily neoplatonism.

10. Cicero, *De Officiis,* trans. Walter Miller (Cambridge, Mass.: Harvard University Press, 1938), p. 127 (1. 34. 125). The translation here is mine, not Miller's.

11. The rustication of Christianity, in the anchorite and monastic movements, of course had begun several decades before Augustine's birth. As the ancient urban fabric decomposed, the ministry of the gospel removed into the countryside, there to set up monasteries. The monastery was, as Lewis Mumford points out, "a new kind of polis," a citadel in which "the ideal purposes of the city were sorted out, kept alive, and eventually renewed." See his *The City in History* (New York: Harcourt Brace & World, 1961), p. 246.

12. Seneca, *Moral Essays,* vol. 2, trans. John W. Basore (New York: G. P. Putnam's Sons, 1932), pp. 187-189.

13. Etienne Gilson, "Foreword" in *The City of God* (New York: Fathers of the Church, Inc., 1950), vol. 1, pp. lxxx-lxxxi.

14. Ibid., p. lxxxi.

15. W. H. Auden, *For the Time Being: A Christmas Oratorio* (New York: Random House, 1944).

16. Philip Sharrard, *Constantinople: Iconography of a Sacred City* (London: Oxford University Press, 1965), p. 44.

17. Gilson, "Foreword" in *The City of God,* pp. lxxxiii-lxxxiv.

18. E. Baldwin Smith, *Architectural Symbolism of Imperial Rome and the Middle Ages* (Princeton, N.J.: Princeton University Press, 1956).

19. Eusebius, *Ecclesiastical History,* vol. 2, with a translation by J. E. L. Oulton (Cambridge, Mass.: Harvard University Press, 1952), pp. 421-445 (10. 4. 37-72).

20. Irwin Panofsky, "Introduction," in *Abbot Suger on the Abbey Church of St.-Denis and Its Art Treasures* (Princeton, N.J.: Princeton University Press, 1946), p. 3.

21. "Urban and the Crusaders," ed. Dana Carleton Munro, in *Translations*

and Reprints from the Original Sources of European History (Philadelphia: Department of History of the University of Pennsylvania, 1897), vol. 1, fasc. 2, pp. 7–8.

22. Did the crusaders remember Urban's words as they perished of hunger and thirst on the march between Antioch and Jerusalem? Dante, writing after ten or twelve crusades had well acquainted Europe with the actual geography and climate of Palestine, constructed a cosmos in which Jerusalem was at the opposite extreme from the Earthly Paradise.

23. W. H. Matthews, *Mazes and Labyrinths: Their History and Development* (New York: Dover, 1970), pp. 54–70. See also Eliade, *Patterns in Comparative Religion,* p. 381: "[Labyrinths] represented, in other words, access to the sacred, to immortality, to absolute reality, by means of initiation. . . . The labyrinth, like any other trial of initiation, is a difficult trial in which not all are fitted to triumph." A familiar form of the "Jerusalem" labyrinth is the hopscotch diagram, whose last space, dome shaped, is called "heaven."

24. George Lesser, *Gothic Cathedrals and Sacred Geometry* (London: Alec Tiranti, 1957); Otto von Simson, *The Gothic Cathedral,* Bollingen Series XLVIII (New York: Pantheon Books, 1956), chs. 1–2.

25. See Joseph Sauer, *Symbolik des Kirchengebäudes* (Freiburg: Herder & Co., 1924), pp. 87–91; Hans H. Hofstatter, *Living Architecture: Gothic,* trans. A. N. Wells (London: Macdonald & Co., 1970), pp. 49–50. Their sources include both fathers of the early church—Jerome, Clement of Alexandria, Tertullian and Athanasius—and medieval theologians such as Hugh of Saint Victor, Sicardus of Cremona, William Duranti, and Honorius of Autun. Panofsky, in *Abbot Suger on the Abbey Church of St.-Denis and Its Art Treasures,* explains that some medieval writers actually called the west front "the north" in order to assimilate into their mythos those demonic forces which Hebrew cosmology had attributed to the dark North (pp. 209–212).

26. Rudolf Schwarz, *The Church Incarnate,* trans. Cynthia Harris (Chicago: Henry Regnery Co., 1958), p. 53. Schwarz's work influenced that of Christian Norberg-Schulz, cited above in reference to the prophets. See ch. 1, n. 9.

27. Ibid., p. 119.

28. Ibid., pp. 135–136.

29. Ibid., pp. 126–127.

3. THE TRIUMPH OF THE MAP

1. Kevin Lynch, *The Image of the City* (Cambridge, Mass.: M.I.T. Press, 1960). Lynch's findings, though, may be skewed by his surveys' indifference to socioeconomic distinctions in his respondents. Other factors than urban "legibility" may explain why the residents of Cambridge are more at ease with their environment, and more articulate about its configuration, than the citizens of Union City and Los Angeles. Further, the kind of imaginative coherence implied by his survey questions may simply be the kind Lynch shares with the citizens of Cambridge.

2. E. Baldwin Smith, *Architectural Symbolism of Imperial Rome and the Middle Ages* (Princeton, N.J.: Princeton University Press, 1956), p. 36.

3. Mircea Eliade, *The Sacred and the Profane,* trans. Willard Trask (1957; reprint ed., New York: Harper & Row, 1961), p. 25. See also Lewis Mumford, *The City in History* (New York: Harcourt Brace and World, 1961), pp. 64–70.

4. *Gilgamesh,* trans. N. K. Sandars (Harmondsworth: Penguin Books, 1960), p. 59. I have set the translation in verse lines.

5. "Romulus," in *Plutarch's Lives,* trans. Bernadotte Perrin (Cambridge, Mass.: Harvard University Press, 1959), p. 119 (x–xi).

6. *Epitome of the Ecclesiastical History of Philostorgius,* trans. Edward Walford (London: H. G. Bohn, 1885), p. 438 (2. 9).

7. Philip Sharrad, *Constantinople: Iconography of a Sacred City* (London: Oxford University Press, 1965), p. 8.

8. In the account of Prudentius's *Psychomachia* in chapter 1, we saw such a mixture of military and religious considerations turned into allegory as a party of Virtues, working as both priests and engineers, turned a Roman defensive encampment into the city where God makes his home.

9. Vitruvius, *The Ten Books on Architecture,* trans. Morris Hicky Morgan (1914; reprint ed., New York: Dover Publications, 1960), pp. 17–31 (1. 4–6).

10. Giulio C. Argan, *The Renaissance City* (New York: George Braziller, 1969), pp. 14–15.

11. Cf. Pierre Lavedan, *Histoire de l'Urbanisme* (Paris: Henri Laurens, 1941), vol. 2, p. 18.

12. Andrea Palladio, *Four Books of Architecture* (New York: Dover Publications, 1965), pp. 59, 72. To Palladio's credit it must be said that his conception of the piazza is not as a *place d'armes* but as a ground for various human intercourse, and that his prisons are designed to be "healthy and commodious" because, he says, their function is not to torment men, but to keep them safe.

13. In her *Theatre of the World* (Chicago: University of Chicago Press, 1969), Frances A. Yates relates the British theaters to the cosmology of Renaissance neoplatonism and the revival of Vitruvian architectural ideals.

14. Pliny the Younger, *Letters and Panegyricus,* with a translation by Betty Radice (Cambridge, Mass.: Harvard University Press, 1959), vol. 2, p. 361 (16. 3).

15. Argan, *Renaissance City,* pp. 25–26. In this age, the architect attained an autocratic preeminence in the building trade, comparable to the prince in the state.

16. René Descartes, *Discourse on Method,* trans. Paul J. Olscamp (Indianapolis, Ind.: Bobbs-Merrill Co., Inc., 1965), pp. 11–13 (2).

17. The concept of several coexistent "spaces" is expressed by Christian Norberg-Schulz in *Existence, Space and Architecture* (New York: Praeger, Inc., 1971).

18. Lavedan, *Histoire de l'Urbanisme,* p. 225.

19. Reginald Blomfield, *Sebastien le Prestre de Vauban* (London: Methuen & Co., 1938), p. 57.

20. Lavedan, *Histoire de l'Urbanisme,* pp. 232–245.

21. *Oeuvres de J. de La Fontaine,* ed. Henri Regnier (Paris: Librairie Hachette, 1890–1929), vol. 8, p. 124.

22. Louis XIV, *Mémoires Historiques et Politiques,* vol. 1 of *Oeuvres de Louis XIV* (Paris: Treuttel and Würtz, 1806), p. 22.

23. Helen M. Fox, *André Le Nôtre: Garden Architect to Kings* (New York: Crown Publishers, 1962), p. 80.

24. La Fontaine, *Oeuvres,* vol. 8, pp. 36, 121.

25. Louis is quoted in Ernest de Ganay, *André Le Nostre* (Paris: Editions Vincent, Fréal & Cie., 1962), pp. 33ff.

26. Derek Clifford, *A History of Garden Design* (New York: Frederick A. Praeger, 1963), p. 73.

27. Richard Wilbur, "Castles and Distances," in *The Poems of Richard Wilbur* (New York: Harcourt Brace Jovanovich, 1963), p. 123.

28. Mumford, *The City in History,* p. 391.

29. Bernini's plan was defeated—in his own time by a failure to complete the colonnade, in the twentieth century by Mussolini's opening a broad avenue from St. Peter's square to the Tiber.

30. Ganay, *André le Nostre,* pp. 12–16.

31. David H. Pinkney, *Napoleon III and the Rebuilding of Paris* (Princeton: Princeton University Press, 1958), pp. 35–36.

32. Quoted in J. M. and Brian Chapman, *The Life and Times of Baron Haussmann* (London: Weidenfeld and Nicholson, 1957), p. 77.

33. Howard Saalman, *Haussmann: Paris Transformed* (New York: George Braziller, 1971), p. 17.

34. An appearance only; skillful composition in the architecture of the new Louvre conceals a skew caused by the original siting of the old Louvre (built in 1202) and of the Tuileries (1564) as independent structures, one within the old city wall and the other without.

35. Chapman and Chapman, *Baron Haussmann,* pp. 175–177. Zola's *Nana* studies the interchangeability of three worlds in the Second Empire: the demi-monde, the theater, and the aristocracy. Set in the theater of Offenbach, the race-track of the renovated Bois de Boulogne, and the stagy new houses on the new boulevards, it begins with the heroine's debut in the popular theater of that epoch and ends with her death in the midst of the war fever immediately preceding Louis Napoleon's melodramatic defeat at Sedan.

36. Albert Speer, *Inside the Third Reich* (New York: The Macmillan Co., 1970), pp. 74–80.

37. Ibid., p. 133.

38. Ibid., p. 153.

39. For an analogy in another medium, see Leni Reifenstahl's film *The Triumph of the Will,* where Hitler's personality is in large degree incorporated with that of the people in their marches and assemblies at the Nürnberg Nazi Party convention.

40. Elizabeth S. Kite, comp., *L'Enfant and Washington* (Baltimore: The Johns Hopkins Press, 1929), pp. 47–48. For a comprehensive history of the development of the American capital, containing L'Enfant's plan and many others, see John W. Reps, *Monumental Washington: The Planning and Development of the Capital Center* (Princeton: Princeton University Press, 1967).

41. If there be any truth, then, to the popular idea that L'Enfant's plan symbolizes the constitution, it must be in imitating not the structure of the federal government but the political effects of it.

42. "The L'Enfant Memorials," *Records of the Columbia Historical Society* 2 (1899): 93.

43. See my essay, "Baroque and Picturesque Motifs in L'Enfant's Design for the Federal Capital," *American Quarterly* 26, no. 1 (March, 1974), 23–36.

44. Henry Adams, *The Education of Henry Adams,* ed. Ernest Samuels (Boston: Houghton Mifflin Co., 1973), p. 367.

45. "Report of the Park Commission," in *The Improvement of the Park System of the District of Columbia,* ed. Charles Moore (Washington, D.C.: U.S. Government Printing Office, 1902), p. 36.

46. *Pennsylvania Avenue: Report of the President's Temporary Commission*

on Pennsylvania Avenue (Washington, D.C.: U.S. Government Printing Office, 1969), p. 66.

47. Ibid., p. 7. The Commission's recommendations extended beyond the beautification of the avenue into practical efforts to revitalize and diversify the adjacent business district. Otherwise the avenue will just become a Potemkin Village in Federal Massive, behind which the decay of the present avenue will reappear a block or two north.

48. Charles Moore, *Daniel Burnham: Architect, Planner of Cities* (1921; reprint ed., New York: Da Capo Press, 1968), vol. 2, p. 147.

4. WHERE WILL THE WORD RESOUND?

1. One of the strongest centers of early Christian belief and theology did arise at Alexandria, the intellectual capital of the Mediterranean world, but it took root there first in that city's large and spiritually vital Jewish community. Alexandria was not just a crossroads of the world's ideas, but a metropolis large enough to sustain an unassimilated subculture among which religious belief could be fostered and propagated. See chapter 5.

2. Saint Augustine, *Confessions,* trans. Rex Warner (New York: Mentor Omega Books, 1963), p. 55 (3. 3), pp. 86–87 (4. 16). I have altered slightly the translation of the latter passage.

3. T. S. Eliot, *Collected Poems 1909–1962* (New York: Harcourt Brace and World, 1963), p. 198.

4. Ibid., p. 92.

5. Ibid., p. 178.

6. Ibid., p. 53. Eliot canceled a line later in this section which referred to the prophetic testimony of John in the Book of Revelation. Later in the poem was another line, also canceled, quoting Plato's *Republic* 9. 592, to the effect that the ideal city is to be found not here, but in another world. See *The Waste Land: A Facsimile and Transcript of the Original Drafts,* ed. Valerie Eliot (New York: Harcourt Brace Jovanovich, 1971), pp. 9, 31.

7. Ibid., p. 75.

8. Eliot had experimented with such an approach in the earlier "Preludes" sequence, in which the speaker's consciousness progressively dissolves into that of his urban surroundings, so that he becomes nothing more than the street he beholds, and the street arises to consciousness, vision, and finally conscience.

9. Martin Buber, *I and Thou,* trans. Ronald Gregor Smith (New York: Charles Scribner's Sons, 1958), pp. 44–45.

10. Kevin Lynch, *The Image of the City* (Cambridge, Mass.: M.I.T. Press, 1960), p. 41. *What Time Is This Place?* (Cambridge, Mass.: M.I.T. Press, 1972) is not so much a description of how citydwellers experience time, but rather a speculative and prescriptive treatment of how Lynch thinks time should be kept by the city.

11. Christian Norberg-Schulz, *Existence, Space and Architecture* (New York: Praeger, Inc., 1971), pp. 35–36.

12. My description depends both on Norberg-Schulz, pp. 10–14 and 20, and on Ernst Cassirer, *The Philosophy of Symbolic Form,* trans. Ralph Manheim (New Haven: Yale University Press, 1953), vol. 2, pp. 83–85.

13. Federico Fellini, *La Dolce Vita,* trans. Oscar DeLiso and Bernard Shir-Cliff (New York: Ballantine Books, 1961); *Eclipse,* trans. Louis Brigante, in *Screenplays of Michelangelo Antonioni* (New York: The Orion Press, 1963). My view of these two films has been enriched by conversations with Professor Donald Costello of the University of Notre Dame.

14. Urban detective movies, particularly the *film noir* of the 1940s, exploit in their own fashion the same view of the city. The detective moves through a scene of labyrinthine duplicity and ambiguity, in which he must expect that every person's motives are absolutely egocentric, and where intellectual confusion is often paralleled by the visual indistinctness and circuitous motion of city streets and corridors. But he knows, and the viewers know, that somewhere in the city is a room where the truth will be told. When those words have been heard, then all the random facts will mesh, and all the crooked ways will be made straight, and the film is at an end. Of course in Antonioni's essays into the detective film, such as *L'Avventura* and *Blow-Up,* the story ravels away without our ever reaching that arcanum of truth.

15. Lewis Mumford, *The City in History* (New York: Harcourt Brace and World, 1961), pp. 543-544.

16. Walt Whitman, "Song of Myself," chant 23; "By Blue Ontario's Shore," chant 15; "Give Me the Splendid Silent Sun"; "Song of Myself," chants 25 and 3; in *Leaves of Grass,* ed. Harold W. Blodgett and Scully Bradley (New York: New York University Press, 1965), pp. 51, 352, 313, 55, 30.

17. Frank Lloyd Wright, *The Living City* (1958; reprint ed., New York: New American Library, 1970), p. 60.

18. Ibid., p. 71.

19. Ibid., p. 240.

20. Mumford, p. 573.

21. Marshall McLuhan, *Understanding Media* (New York: McGraw-Hill, 1965), pp. 67-68.

22. Gabriel Marcel, *Man Against Mass Society,* trans. G. S. Fraser (1952; reprint ed., Chicago: Henry Regnery Co., 1962), p. 139.

23. Buber, *I and Thou,* p. 62.

24. Ibid., pp. 67-68.

25. Eliot, *Collected Poems,* p. 62 (*The Waste Land,* ll. 249-256).

26. Ibid., p. 57 (ll. 126-128). The "Shakespearian Rag" was a popular ragtime tune of the postwar era.

27. John Dos Passos, *Manhattan Transfer* (Boston: Houghton Mifflin, 1953), pp. 352-353.

28. Whitman, "Crossing Brooklyn Ferry," *Leaves of Grass,* p. 160.

29. Allen Ginsberg, *Planet News 1961-1967* (San Francisco: City Lights Books, 1968), pp. 117-121.

30. Ibid., p. 127.

5. BETWEEN PENTECOST AND MILLENNIUM

1. See John McKenzie, S.J., *Dictionary of the Bible* (New York: The Bruce Publishing Co., 1965), pp. 155, 550. "She is my wife and I am her husband from this day forever," says an ancient Jewish marriage formula.

2. The term is William Lynch's; see ch. 6 of *Christ and Apollo* (1960; reprint ed., Notre Dame, Indiana: University of Notre Dame Press, 1975). Its discriminated use here, however, is not quite Lynch's.

3. Jacques Ellul, *The Meaning of the City*, trans. Dennis Pardee (Grand Rapids, Michigan: William B. Eerdmans Publishing Co., 1970), pp. 132–133. I have inverted the order of Ellul's sentences, to regain a logic lost by abridgment.

4. Ibid., p. 209.

5. The oldest architectural remains of a Christian church suggest that different parts of the structure were reserved for specific roles or ministries: the clergy closest to the altar, beyond them the baptized laity, usually divided by sex, and at a further distance—indeed in a separate but connecting room—the catechumens, those unbaptized but aspiring to membership. See Richard Krautheimer, *Early Christian and Byzantine Architecture* (Harmondsworth, Middlesex: Penguin Books, 1965), pp. 6–7.

6. Martin Buber, *I and Thou*, trans. Ronald Gregor Smith (New York: Charles Scribner's Sons, 1958), p. 45.

7. Ibid., pp. 113–114.

8. Martin Buber, *Paths in Utopia*, trans. R. F. C. Hull (Boston: Beacon Press, 1958), p. 73.

9. Buber, *I and Thou*, pp. 114–115. Note how Buber invokes the ancient cosmological linking of man, temple, and universe—but here not as a closed sacred space set in a profane world, but rather as the open city of Isaiah 60 and Revelations 21, which makes holy all those who enter into it.

10. Rudolf Schwarz, *The Church Incarnate*, trans. Cynthia Harris (Chicago: Henry Regnery Co., 1958), p. 127.

11. Buber, *I and Thou*, p. 95. In the opening sections of *I and Thou*, Buber's "two primary words" are clearly metaphors for alternative postures of spirit, in no necessary sense verbal. The world of relation, he observes, is threefold: with nature, inarticulate but approaching speech; with man, realized in speech; and with spiritual beings, again without speech but begetting it. Man's dialogue with God is not carried on by the mutual exchange of spoken words. However, in the later pages of this book "word" and "speech" become less metaphoric; as Buber says in the passage quoted above, the spirit's primal act is indeed language and dialogue; of the "gates leading into the presence of the Word," the loving speech of human beings is the main portal: "the moments of relation are here, and only here, bound together by means of the element of the speech in which they are immersed" (pp. 101–103).

12. Buber, *Paths in Utopia*, pp. 135–136.

13. W. H. Auden, *Nones* (New York: Random House, 1951), p. 44.

14. W. H. Auden, *Collected Shorter Poems 1927–1957* (New York: Random House, 1967), pp. 323–338.

15. W. H. Auden, "The Poet and the City," in *The Dyer's Hand* (New York: Random House, 1962), pp. 82–83.

16. Cf. Walter J. Ong, S.J., "Voice as Summons for Belief," in *The Barbarian Within* (New York: Macmillan, 1962), p. 56:

All communication—and, indeed, all our thinking, which is learned and developed only through communication with others—goes on in a context of belief. For when we speak, we invite response. If I expect no response, no Yes, no No, no riposte of any sort, at least internal, I do not normally speak at all. . . . Now, any expectation of response is in some way a declaration of belief in

the person or persons to whom I address myself. It is recognition of a presence to whose word I can, in turn, attend, and in whom I can thus believe through the acceptance of what he has to say.
See also T. S. Eliot's *Burnt Norton*: "My words echo / Thus, in your mind." To several courses from Father Ong, at St. Louis University, I owe many of the seminal ideas of this book.

17. Gabriel Marcel, *Man Against Mass Society*, trans. G. S. Fraser (1952; reprint ed., Chicago: Henry Regnery Co., 1962), pp. 89–90.

18. Ibid., p. 44. At about the same time, Albert Camus was describing the Stalinist betrayal of Marxism in a similar image: "In the kingdom of humanity [lit., 'of persons'], men are bound by ties of affection; in the Empire of objects, men are united by mutual accusation. The city that planned to be the city of fraternity becomes an ant-heap of solitary men" (*The Rebel*, trans. Anthony Bower [New York: Vintage Books, 1956], p. 239).

19. Marcel, pp. 146–147, 206, 267.

20. Ibid., pp. 189–191.

21. Perhaps the failure of many isolated restricted families and of most modern communes stems both from an unrealistic demand for continuously affirmative and continuously "I-Thou" relationships and from the absence of any prior faith on which the members' contingent faith in one another can be grounded.

22. Karl Rahner, "The Christian in his World," in *Theological Investigations VII; Further Theology of the Spiritual Life,* vol. 1, trans. David Bourke (New York: Herder and Herder, 1971), pp. 88–99.

23. Schwarz, *The Church Incarnate,* p. 228.

24. Rahner, p. 91. In these words lingers Augustine's conviction that the only true *civitas* would be one composed exclusively of those who hear and follow the word of God.

25. Buber, *Paths in Utopia,* p. 75. The Roman Catholic Church recently sacrificed most of a generation of liberal and socially conscientious men and women whose imaginations, nurtured on a millennial city, had not been educated in such recognitions.

26. Buber, *I and Thou,* p. 54.

27. Rahner, p. 98. "Aber Stil, Verhaltensmuster, konkrete Leitbilder . . . müssen . . . ausgebildet werden."

28. Therefore, it is possible that the analogical imagination may leave few literary traces of its activity, preferring the spoken word and its invitation into action to the written word reduced to an aesthetic object.

Index

Acts of the Apostles, 91-92, 125-31
Alaric, 25, 154 (n. 3)
Alien. *See* Exile; and *Peregrinus*.
Alienation, 104-06, 114-15, 138-40
Allegory. *See* Exegesis; and Imagination, allegorical.
Analogy. *See* Imagination, analogical.
Antonioni, Michelangelo, 102, 104-07, 160 (n. 14)
Apocalypse, 42, 143; in Augustine, 30; modern, 95-98, 104, 106, 108, 117; in NT, 16-22, 133-34; in OT, 8-15, 17-18; Roman, 154 (n. 11). *See also* Eschatology; Millennium; and Revelation (NT).
Apocalypse, The (NT). *See* Revelation (NT). *See also* Apocalypse; Eschatology; and Millennium.
Aristotle, 54, 63, 65
Auden, W.H., 23, 42, 136-38, 140, 146
Auerbach, Erich, 29-30
Augustine, Saint: *The City of God*, 23-44, 86, 104, 138, 141-42, 144, 155 (n. 9), 162 (n. 24); *The Confessions*, 31-33, 37, 92-94
Axis Mundi. See Center, cosmological.

Babylon. *See* Cities, Babylon.
Bible. (NT) *See* Acts of the Apostles; Epistles; Gospels; and Revelation. (OT) *See* Prophets; and Psalms.
Bonaparte, Louis (Napoleon III), 73-75
Bonaparte, Napoleon (Napoleon I), 73, 113

Bradley, F.H., 98, 100, 115
Buber, Martin, 99, 103, 113, 117, 124, 132, 134-36, 138-41, 146-47, 161 (n. 9, 11)
Burnham, Daniel, 80-82, 84-85

Caesar (title). *See* King.
Camus, Albert, 162 (n. 18)
Cathedral. *See* Church, building; and Churches.
Center: cosmological, 1-7, 22, 24-25, 38, 48-50, 56-60, 65, 69-70, 77, 82, 84, 110, 117, 125, 142-44, 150; cynosure as, 13-17, 35-37, 117; ego as, 98-101, 107-19; loss of, 99-118, 139; visual eminence at, 63-86; word as, 90, 93, 99, 101-03, 105, 107-08, 117-18, 134-36, 139-42, 146-48, 150-51. *See also* City; and Community.
Charlemagne, 44, 46-47, 144
Christ, 15-16, 18-20, 23-53 *passim*, 54, 59, 86, 90-91, 94, 104, 125, 132, 138, 142-43, 145-51; as Word, 86, 93, 122-25
Church: in Acts of the Apostles, 125-31; building, 20-22, 32, 36, 43-46, 49-53, 144-45, 148, 161 (n. 5) (*See also* Churches; and Space, sacred); as community, 21-22, 32-33, 122-34, 138, 142-51 (*See also* Community); corporate image in Saint Paul, 32, 131-33, 147; as counter-kingdom, 16-19, 31-36, 39-43, 46-47 (*See also* City, as fortress); in Epistles, 16-17, 130-34; as institution, 35-36, 130-35, 144-46, as

163